BLUE LIES

(Reality Changes the Hustle of the Game)

———————

(D. L. REYNOLDS)

BLUE LIES

(Reality Changes the Hustle of the Game)

By

D. L. Reynolds

ACKNOWLEDGMENTS

All the hustlers, young and old, dead or alive, who just happen to leave a legacy of life lessons for all of us to live and learn by, but hopefully helps us to make wiser choices in all that we do and plan on doing.

BLUE LIES

(Reality Changes the Hustle of the Game)

By D. L. Reynolds

Dedication

To all the young hustlers of this and future societies; choose your path in accordance to the way of prosperity without stepping on others and engaging in negative activities to achieve ultimate success and the reward will undoubtedly free the way for you to bless others more worthy than yourself. Be more positive in your thinking and doing for the sake of all mankind.

Chapter One

My boy Onyx and I had been thick as thieves since the age of two, and the only times that we were apart was when I had to be with my mom as an Army brat. Every day was a new adventure, and by the time we had reached middle school age, Onyx had befriended a guy named Theo Eubanks, who went by the name "Eubie." Eubie was a cool guy, sort of loud from time to time, and he also had a quick temper, but other than that, we all got along very well, at least for the first for a few months.

By mid-June, me, Onyx, and Eubie had been hanging together every day, but after Eubie's cousin Saigon was found dead in a rundown apartment building. "Hustle Run," which is a neighborhood full of minority families, especially Blacks, and an instant playground for drug dealers, junkies, thieves, and perverts, and just 2 buildings down, many single family houses and duplexes sit directly across the streets from a liquor store, meat market, and three more bungalow-styled houses; the owner of stores and laundry mat lives in the first house. Eubie became somewhat distant and cold, and me and Onyx couldn't figure out why for nothing.

"Man, what is going on with Eub?" Onyx shouted.

"You got me by the balls man," I replied. "Ever since he been running numbers and weed for Big Scout, his whole attitude shifted."

"Man, every time I see him, a tall, slim dude with braids is following his every move and he watches him from across the street and stand between buildings," Eubie said. He continued, "I also heard that Mylo keep tabs on him everywhere he goes because Big Scout don't trust nobody, especially teen-agers."

Since age of eight, me, Eubie and Onyx hung out together all of the time except during the times when I had to travel with my mom, but every time she went on temporary duty or places where I could not go, she left me in the care of my great aunt Eunice. Aunt Eunice was the sister of my mom's mother, or so I was told; turns out, Eunice Bea Williams was a former prostitute who sort of adopted my granny as her little sister a long time ago, but why, I was unsure until later on in life. But, if any one knew the true story, or anything close to the truth, Ms. Duby did; this woman saw all and knew all about everything and everybody.

At that moment, we got a glimpse of Ms. Duby peeking out of her front door, then moving towards her favorite spot in a big chair on her open porch where she watch and listen to everything going on in the neighborhood.

"Hey Ms. Duby, how you doing today?" I shouted as Eubie waved.

"Ms. Duby always doing fine, but what you two youngsters doing hanging out on that curb over there? "Y'all need to find something productive to do and stay outta these here streets looking and waiting where trouble come," she snapped.

"Come over here for a minute boy," she looked dead at me and motioned me to come over; meanwhile, Eubie looked at me with a slight grin, and quickly said, "Well man, you on yo' own, I am getting up outta here fo' she motioned me over there, cause you know she finna talk you to death so I will see you later at Skeet's," then he left.

"Boy, dontcha know that there boy Eubie ain't no good and he sho ain't yo' friend," she scolded. "How long fo yo' momma get back from over them seas and come get yo' butt, cause all I see is that you gon catch it out here in these here streets hanging out with that boy Eubie and Onyx." Onyx got mo shit going on than he can handle, and fo you know it, his troubles gon come knocking at you and Eubie's door, so you need to distant yo 'self from both of 'em." "I know you thank Eubie is a good friend, but I tell you, that boy thank he is slick as wet rain on a highway, with his sneaky ass, and that Onyx, you and Eubie been seeing changes in him, and they ain't good cause he gon get hurt or sent to jail soon 'cause you can't tell that no good boy nothing." All I could do is say yes, ma'am, and keep listening without saying too much unless she asked me to speak cause that's how I was raised. "My mom will be back in July then we will be going to Fort Bragg in North Carolina or Virginia, I'm not sure yet," I told her.

She quickly looked me straight in the eyes without blinking and said, "Keep yo nose clean, cause if I catch you doing wrong, it won't be pretty." Then, she stated, "And as fo friends, don't count on 'em and don't make too many cause folks cain't be trusted and they lie to your face and hide a lot of important stuff, so take people for what they show you and how they talk about other folk, especially they kinfolk." "Now gon on back over cross them tracks and check on yo' Aunt Eunice cause she be having something fo you to do right about now," she shouted.

Although I thought Ms. Duby was a mean busybody, I also realized that she knew a lot more about life than I did, and whenever you get the chance to listen to her up close, she makes a whole lot of sense. Furthermore, I was always taught to respect people, especially the elders, and looking back on those days, I appreciate a lot of them one-on-one talks with Ms. Duby, but as a kid, I dreaded talking to.

So, as I got closer to my Aunt Eunice's house, I saw a nice black, brand new 1971 Cadillac Coupe De Ville parked right behind it, and a '71 mint green Cadillac

Broham, and a nut brown '71 Lincoln Continental parked right in front of the house. My first thought was that something bad had happened, but for a long minute, I was too fascinated with the beauty of these cars. As I got closer to the Lincoln, my Aunt Eunice yelled from the front door, "Boy, where you been?" I sent that boy Womp to find you 'bout twenty minutes ago, then he never showed back up," she added.

"They found Dayo and Stank Man tied up and beaten up in Mr. Schlonke's Dry Cleaning sto down on Banks Avenue, and they claim the two boys was trying to rob him this morning, but they cain't find Mr. Schlonke nowhere, so I called Erb to see what was going on and if you was anywhere near this shit." Erb was Aunt Eunice's nephew and a well-respected pimp and hustler; he owned the new black Caddie, and his colleagues were fellow hustlers Mint and Scat.

I told her who I was with and then I got a long lecture from the men anyway about how I need to be more careful out on the street. After listening to everyone scold me I went to my room, I overheard them talking about how Mr. Schlonke wasn't robbed, he was on the run cause they learned that he had been messing with young boys and threatening to lie about them trying to rob him if they ever told anyone. Ms. Martha and her niece Charlene had entered the cleaners and notice that Mr. Schlonke's fingers had something on them and he smelled pretty bad; also, his pants were unzipped. So, when Ms. Martha asked how come his zipper was undone and why was he shaking so bad, he told her that he had just left the bathroom, but Charlene spotted Stank Man's shoes and socks near the side entry way, and asked him about them. At that moment, he excused himself and ran towards the front door, and Charlene suspected fowl play and as she peaked around the counter, she heard faint sounds of someone trying to speak. Ms. Martha told her not to go back there, but she went any way, and that's when she discovered the boys.

"Let's get these boys outta here, and once we make it to Carla's house, we gone call the police," Charlene said. "All we gotta do is call and say that we found some little boy's underwear all around the cleaners, along with tape, hand-cuffs, and dirty magazines, but that nobody was working in the store," she went on. They did find this stuff in the back where they found the boys, so before they left the store, they placed these items all around the front part of the store so the police could find them.

"Thank goodness we got there when they did because Mr. Schlonke didn't get the chance to actually hurt these two boys, Ms. Martha told them, but once the police searched the cleaners and the upstairs apartment of Mr. Schlonke, they found more evidence that he had been molesting little boys and a notebook that explained how he had killed and buried two of them. Furthermore, the police discovered that the two dead boys were those who had gone missing about three years ago when everyone thought they had run away; the boys were twelve at the time. The remains of the two boys were found in a trunk hidden under a pile of thick blankets.

The parents of the two dead boys were devastated because they had to relive this episode all over again. No one ever found Mr. Schlonke, but from what people in the neighborhood was saying, Mr. Schlonke had somehow left the country and was now living in Europe somewhere. The truth is, according to what Scat told Aunt Raina, his boys had located Mr. Schlonke hiding at his cousin Mr. Friedham's house in the basement. Once they entered Mr. Friedham's home, they discovered three Black boys who looked like they were between the ages of seven and ten, sitting on a couch in pajamas. All hell broke loose and the guys grabbed both Mr. Friedham and Mr. Schlonke and Loody and Ray stuffed them in the car; no one has ever heard from either man since that day. The three boys were taken to their relatives who discovered that one of them had been sexually abused while the other two were ordered to watch and wait their turn.

To this day, according to Scat, no one mention either man, and as far as the dry cleaners store goes, a long lost niece of Mr. Schlonke's wanted to claim ownership, but was forced by a hustler by the name of Huey Dunn, to turn it over to him along with the house owned by Mr. Friedham. Furthermore, Mr. Friedham's home consisted of more evidence of the two men's dirty deeds, but for some reason, the police never learned about this information, and frankly, no one cared. Huey turned the house into a gambling joint which is still operating to this day.

All I could do is wonder how if something like this happened to me and my friends, would we be found before harm could be done to us. Man, I feel sorry for those little boys and their families, and this discussion made me realize how crazy some people are.

After the men had left, Aunt Eunice called me into the dining room I knew I was in for a long lecture, so I braced myself to get scold as well, and sure enough, soon as I entered the room, she lit into me again. "Boy, I don't care if you in the bathroom and taking too long, you better holler out and let me know where you are and what you doing, you hear me? She scolded. I shook my head in agreement, but she thumped me on the forehead and said, "Don't be nodding yo head to me, you better say yes ma'am, cause as long as you can speak, you better and leave all that head nodding to them people who cain't talk at all," she continued.

"You know yo mom won't like it if you do wrong, and I don't want her to thank that I cain't handle you, cause she knows that I will spank that butt if I have to, you hear me?"

I quickly answered, "Yes, Ma'am."

Well, after that fiasco, I hung out with Eubie later on that day, and as we were sitting and talking about the days' events, Saigon and Woo Man showed up. "Hey Sai," Eubie cried. "Where y'all been?"

"Down by Lakes Road where the night hustlers hang out until they go out in the streets," he offered. He added, "Man, them cats be on a serious mission when it comes to planning strategies for making money 'cause they don't only run drugs and numbers, they also help with body counts from the big dogs." "Jubie and Ant was down there in the dungeon with them and from what we saw, he wasn't playing about Big Tate's money that one of Ant's runners had messed up......they made us scram cause I thank they was getting ready to do some serious damage to them cats." We ran down to Florence and hung around there until we passed all of the Jaded corners of Rock's end of town, then we came up here."

Tray Dog and Limp warned us to lay low from this area for a while cause the steam was getting too hot and innocent people might get cause up in all the chaos that was brewing. So me and Eubie took their advice literally.

Every once in a while, the older cats will allow me, Eubie, Saigon, and Woo Man come into their circle during the day hours so we can see how their planning techniques go, but, they also had hidden agendas; these cats were already trying to plan our destiny cause they looked at us as future runners and hustlers, but the big man of the house called Bird, wasn't so sure 'bout Saigon and Woo Man. In fact, he told me and Eubie that he trusts us now but don't thank he'll ever completely trust the other two cause they seem a bit elusive and shady. Bird also told us that time will be revealed real soon about these two cause they gone do a test run on them since they were older than me and Eubie.

Two weeks after this talk, Woo Man came up missing, so Saigon hid out for about a whole month.

But, once he resurfaced, a woman of the streets named Letta Pearl found him badly beaten behind a dumpster on Road Street close to where she was dropped off by a john. Saigon told us that Woo Man had stolen $7900.00 from the money he collected and tried to blame on him. Although the Cards, (One of Stick Man's crew that handled the west end of town), learned that Saigon was telling the truth, they beat him just to set an example and to warn him of what could have been worse. "Man, after they kicked my ass, they forced Woo Man in the trunk of Red's car, then sped off down towards the docks," he shakenly explained. He also stated that "And when the prostitute tried to help me, her pimp, Tooter came up and started yelling at her and slapping her shouting, Bitch, you supposed to be out on yo post making money, what you doin' round here for?" "But once he realized I was on the ground, he motioned for his main thrower called Big Ox to come and put me in his car." He also added, "Once I was in Tooter's car, he told me that he had heard on the streets about what happened and that I need to forget about Woo Man and go into hiding for a while; then, he dropped me off at one of his apartments on Friars Court, and told me to stay there until he gives me the word in about a month or so, and that one of his women would be making sure that I get food and other necessities."

The funny thing about all of this is that Saigon didn't know, at that time, that Tooter, a.k.a. Wenton Mason, Jr., was his eldest brother who had served in Vietnam, but was once a heroin addict that caused their overly religious parents to disown him. Tooter, however, knew who Saigon was and he made sure that he looked out for his little brother; he later told him the whole truth about who he was a couple of weeks later, and their bond has been golden ever since. He sent Saigon to college, then talked him into going in the military halfway through school, but Saigon did get his associate degree.

So, as I sit here and travel backwards to revisit where I have been and how I made it to be here today, I realize that no matter what life and people appear to be, there is always a story behind a story, and many can erupt the lives of unsuspecting members of families, circles of friends, and even your enemies. One things for sure, if it looks too good, then it may be deadly in the end.

Chapter Two

Well, several months had passed since the Saigon fiasco and Eubie and I thought that things were kind of getting back to normal until school started. Although I may not be able to complete the entire school year because my mom is expected back in the states around Thanksgiving time, I decided to make the best of things while I'm here.

Eubie and I had started off well at the beginning of school, but somewhere things took a crazy turn in the middle of September. Eubie had started skipping school at least three times a week and missing band practice; Eubie plaid the flute and bass while I plaid the saxophone; also, besides the sax, I played piano, bass guitar, and drums, but for the school band, I focused on one instrument, the sax.

"Eubie man, what are you doing?" I asked.

"What do you mean man?" he replied.

"Why are you missing so much school and band practice?" "I thought you wanted to improve your grades and make a bigger effort to do better in school than you did last year; what's going on with you?

"Nothing much man, but I know you cain't make no money if you don't go where the money-making opportunities is!" he offered.

I just looked at him in great disbelieve cause evidently, he didn't learn much from the stuff that happened during the summer, especially with Saigon and Woo Man. I decided that although this has been my right hand man since day one, and we always had each other's back for years, knowing Eubie like I do, once he makes his mind up about something, that's it. All I can do is hope that he won't regret his decisions, and frankly, I really don't want to know nothing about who he's working for and what he's actually doing.

"If you wasn't so much of a punk, you'd be rolling with me so we can make this money together cause you know we a tag team when we doing anything," he stated sarcastically. I tried my best to ignore him and not reply at all 'cause I didn't need all the drama that I could see coming from this.

Ever since that day when I had that short conversation with Eubie a huge and fearful feeling has settled in the pit of my stomach. Thinking of Aunt Eunice and my mom's warnings, *"When something about someone close to you doesn't feel right, then usually, it isn't."* When I arrived at Aunt Eunice's house, I told her about the conversation I had with Eubie and how he's been skipping school and band practice, and she just looked up to the ceiling for at least five minutes before speaking.

"Well, honey, it's time for you to start distancing yo 'self from that boy 'cause I feel danger ahead and the results ain't pretty," she said. "Furthermore, if he been skipping school like you say, then keeping secrets from you should tell you more than what you think," she added.

"When people start changing their habits and keeping stuff from the ones who they been around for a very long time, then it can only show you that whatever they doing, it ain't good; however, Eubie must value y'all's friendship more than you think cause if he didn't, he would've tried to get you involved with what he's doing from the get-go," she continued. "Now if you keep on him 'bout this thang then he gon start lying to you cause he already know you ain't trying to get into what he's doing, cause chile, he's already lying to himself to believe that quick money gon solve all his problems, for just as quick as he get it, he gon spend it even quicker, and the need for more is gon keep growing like a tape worm, cause once folk get a taste for certain thangs, they become greedy and sooner or later they get stupid and do something that can not only bring harm to them but it can harm other folk around them, so, stay away from that boy, you hear me?"

she ended her lecture with returning to the kitchen to check on her corn bread and I went in the room, lied on the bed in deep thought, trying to make sense of it all. I didn't want to break ties completely with my friend, but at the rate he was going, and with the gut-feeling I had about it, I knew my Aunt Eunice was right, but, I wanted to save my boy from himself.

The next day in school, I got with T-Boy and Wade, they were sophomores, and T-Boy was Eubie's first cousin, while Wade was T-Boy's best friend. I thought that the three of us could get Eubie to see reason and get back on the right track, and both of them agreed to do something about this situation.

"Yo T, if yo cuz is hanging with Straws and Felix, they gon' try to get him hooked on Heroin cause they doin' it," Wade said. "Further mo man, if we gon make that move, we gotta get goin' and plan our strategy right cause we gotta go in knowin' what we doing," he continued, "Bae Ray got some info on the situation, so we need to hook up wit him like right now; we can go down to his crib after school 'round five."

As soon as we got out of school, Wade told us to meet him at Hustlin' Joe's joint out on Burbourn Avenue and enter through the side door and ask for Carol. Once we knocked on the door, this gorgeous, medium-caramel skinned woman with finger-waved hair that came down to her shoulders, opened the door and once she opened her mouth to beckon us in, I almost fainted; as beautiful as she looked, her mouth was so jacked up that it resembled bits of bark from a tree branch. T-Boy almost laughed out loud, but found a way to contain himself as she motioned us to a blue and ivory sofa. The first thing I noticed was that this room had no windows and if you looked at the outside building, you'd never know that the inside was a beautiful as it was. This place has so many priceless items in it and whomever decorated it, they made it look like something out of a Queen Ann catalog. Carol was Hustlin' Joe's new find, and by looking at her, I am sure that if I ever get the chance to see her again, all of her flaws, especially that mouth of hers, will look nothing less than perfect, 'cause he was known for taken women that no one else paid attention to and changing their entire presence.

Once we were all seated, Cass, one of Joe's big enforcers appeared; this dude had a face that made you stand in a frozen position and pray that he wouldn't move closer in your direction. "Hey young bloods," Cass said with no emotion. We spoke and sit quietly, waiting for the next words to come out of his mouth, but just as he was about ready to speak again, Motion Ed walked in; he was Hustlin' Joe's top man, and he was more pleasant in his greetings that Cass was.

"Joe told me to let you boys know that the situation is being taken care of, but he also said that y'all need to lay low and refrain from looking for Eubie until he sends word to you," He offered. "I will personally find you and let you know what yo' next move will be, so with that said, I want y'all to go on like normal and let us handle this 'cause there is a lot mo shit involved with this thang then y'all know 'bout, and I don't want y'all to get caught up in this mess."

So, with that said, we headed out and decided to lay low for a bit, but I had a strange notion that something 'bout this whole thing wasn't right, and I spoke on it to T-Boy and Wade. "My gut says that this thing has too many twists and turns and I believe that a whole lot of these gaps in this mess is getting wider and wider, and we being played for fools."

"I so agree with you man, 'cause everyone was too damn calm for one thing," T-Boy claimed. "And that goon Cass being the first to come in automatically spoke volumes, and I thank we being played as pawns 'cause they already know we gon' still do our own investigation."

"Right, and we need to be ready for anything and that means that we shouldn't go nowhere without all of us knowing where we at," Wade stated. "I'm gon talk to Menchie and see what he knows 'cause he always keeps his ears to the streets." Menchie was a weird cat but he knew about everything that was going on out here; they say he was into men, frankly Asian men, but by seeing him on any given day, no one could tell 'cause he looked more manly than any man I know. We all agreed and decided to sleep on it.

Soon as I made it home, Aunt Eunice told me that Marissa had 'came by to seem. Marissa Wright was a sophomore in school, and although I was only a freshman, she was sweet on me, and to be honest, she wasn't bad at all. She had beauty, brains, and a body; the three "B's." She also had a good attitude, unlike many of the freshmen girls did. We hadn't got close enough to go all the way yet, 'cause I still had to get past the words of my Aunt Eunice, "Boy, you get out there and mess around with them lil nasty ass gals and catch something, or worse, getting one of 'em pregnant, I'm gon beat the hell outta you, and so is yo' mama."

"If you gon' be out there doin' somethin' I don't want to know nothin' about it, but you better get something to protect yo 'self." Man, I hate them long and crazy lectures, even though I know she right, I just hate listening to them. There are a lot of girls in school that will sleep with anybody, and many of them get pregnant, graduate to being a hooker, or getting on drugs, or all three and more, and I learned from Erb and other men that just 'cause it looks good, don't trust it like it won't burn you.

On the other hand, I used to like this chick named Telita, but she transferred to another school last year, and from what I heard, she had a baby by a twenty year-old a few months ago. Telita was two years older than me, but she had been held back a couple of grades 'cause she was real sick when she was little. I don't know why it is, but most of the girls that are older than I am approach me more often than they do my boys Eubie, Wade, and T-Boy.

I called Marissa when I got to my room and she told me to come over 'cause she was home alone. Since I was still tripping on the situation with Eubie, I figured this would take my mind off of things, at least for a good minute, so I jetted to her house. When I arrived at Marissa's house, her mom, dad, and older sister Marie were sitting in the living room. I stood at the door a bit puzzled cause Marissa had told me that she was home alone. In fact, I had only been inside of her house once before today, but her family were home at that time.

"Come on in and have a seat, "Mr. I wanna be a grown man," Mrs. Wright said with a real snotty way. I was flabbergasted 'cause I didn't know what was going on. Marissa was sitting in a chair off to the right, holding her head down, and saying nothing; she didn't even say hello when I entered the room.

"Boy, did you knock my baby girl up?" Mr. Wright shouted with a heavy and mean voice. At that moment, I wanted to disappear 'cause I thought this big dude was gon' come over and start pounding on me. I froze. I couldn't say nothing. I looked at Marissa, hoping that she would say something, anything, but she just kept her head down.

I don't know where the courage came from, but I knew that I had to do something quick. "This is only my second time inside of your house, and Marissa has never been to my house, and as far as getting her pregnant, the only thing we ever did was kiss." "I don't know what Marissa told y'all, but I didn't do it."

"You lil punk, he said you would say some bullshit like that," Mr. Wright shouted angrily, then tried to forge his way towards me, but Mrs. Wright interrupted. "I will kill this lil nigger, who he thank he is coming in my house acting like he somebody big enough to lie to my face?"

Just then, Marie came out of Marissa's room, holding her diary shouting, "Daddy, leave him alone, cause he's telling the truth." "Marissa wrote about how she and him never did nothing but kiss, even though she tried to get him to go farther, but she also wrote in here 'bout how she been sneaking out to see Burb Hollister at least three times a week; she also explained how Marissa wrote how long they had been having sex, from the beginning to now, and that she thought she was pregnant by him."

Marissa finally held her head up and scolded, "Yeah daddy, somebody other than you been doing stuff to me." Her daddy stopped in his tracks then ran out of the room and slammed the basement door so hard, that the vase on the mantle fell and splattered into pieces all over the floor, just missing me by a couple of inches.

Mrs. Wright suddenly burst into tears, Marie also added how their dad had been molesting her as well, ever since she was around the age of eleven. I thought about turning around and running, but, all of a sudden, we heard two gunshots coming from the basement.

"Oh Lord, what has Fred don gon and did now?" Mrs. Wright screamed. Me and Marie tried to hold her back from going down in the basement when their brother Silas rushed in 'cause he had head the gunshots too. Silas had left his car running as soon as he drove into the driveway and ran inside. No one was worried about neighbors cause the McKay's' house was at least two or three houses apart from theirs, and the Grimm's' across the street were out of town, so no one else around heard anything.

Silas motioned me to go turn his car off and then come back to go check on his dad. Once we got downstairs, I wanted to throw-up and run out of there, quick. Mr. Wright had shot himself in the mouth two times, and blood was everywhere. His body sat slumped in the chair as his head was cocked back and hanging to the left, and blood was running out of his mouth, and down his neck. This was my first, but not my last time seeing someone who either killed themselves or was killed by someone else and it left me a bit shaken. Silas ordered me to go home and never repeat anything about the events that had just occurred to no one. I agreed and got the hell out of there.

Dang, nothing gets past Aunt Eunice. Sometimes I think she turns into a fly so she can be everywhere that something is happening at. Before I could get in the house good, she met me at the back door and gave me this, "I been telling yo' butt to be mo careful and always be aware of what's goin' on around you," look. "I already know what happened 'cause you know Bett already called and told me everything," she said. Mrs. Wright's first name is Bett, and she and Aunt Eunice have been knowing each other since forever. "Now, just put all that shit out of yo' mind and gon' inside, wash yo' hands and sit down and eat," Aunt Eunice continued. I did just that, and was still kind of shocked, I decided to take a bath and lie down and watch some TV for the rest of the night, even though it was still early and not dark yet.

Weeks passed by and I hadn't been seeing Marissa in school, and I wondered how she was doing. One day, as I was coming out of Flip's Market, I ran into her sister Marie. "Hey Dee, how ya been doing?" I returned the greeting, and before I asked about Marissa, she offered, "Well, I am so sorry that you had to witness all that craziness, but, it turned out that Marissa wasn't pregnant after all and because of everything that happened, my mom sent her to Alabama to stay with my Uncle Irvin and his wife until she graduates from high school, and hopefully, she will stay on down there and go to college cause ain't much here for her but trouble." I agreed, and kept it moving.

Chapter Three

As time went on, Eubie finally stopped coming to school altogether and the weird thing about all of this, he also stopped communicating with me. I became more concerned about my friend, so one Saturday, I stopped by his mom's house around ten in the morning, hoping that he would be there and more than likely still in the bed. Before I could knock on the door, his mom opened it and came out on the porch, motioning me to have a seat. Immediately, I became nervous cause I had a feeling that something was terribly wrong.

"Dee, I ain't seen or heard from my child in about three weeks until two days ago, handing me a mink coat that had ten thousand dollars, the deed to this house, and the paid receipts to all my bills in the side pocket," she said. "I slapped that boy so hard that my hand turned red as a firecracker and Bull had to come between us 'cause I was ready to kill 'em," she managed through light tears and trembling. "That's my youngest baby, but I would kill him dead to save his soul if I had to." "I gave him the wad of money back, but I kept the deed and receipts cause although I did not want no parts of whatever he don got hisself into, I ain't fully stupid either, but I also got in touch with my brother Chase in New York so he can send his boys to get him and keep him from getting too deep in this shit out here in these here streets." Chase was a former pimp/hustler that retired from the game and now lives very well in New York. Although he is supposed to be out of the game, I can't tell 'cause he still has a lot of ties with many of the major players, even those who own legitimate businesses nationwide.

Unfortunately, before Chase could gather his men and scoop Eubie up, my friend got in deep shit with a hustler named Spin. Spin had brought Eubie into his fold, but he also had Dupont; Dupont was the top dog when it came to running for the big hustlers, and he played a serious game of chance with at least four known major hustlers, but had an enemy in one of the spots that was his main competition.

Everyone involved with these hustlers were competing for the top spot, and many of them would set the knee runners, (the runners who are a notch up from the newbies), just to get ahead. Running was a hard hustle in itself, it was also dangerous if you pissed the wrong person off, in which many knee runners did. Scoop was a newbie, running for Big Tiny, but had street and game knowledge from being a major runner for White Face; he had seven years under his belt. White Face and all of his top dogs, and at least seventy-five percent of his runners got set up by Biscuit's people and their bodies were found burned up and shot up in one of his main houses down on Lennox and Quake Run Streets about two years ago. Snake, El, Grinch, and Scoop got lucky as hell that night 'cause they had to make a run down to Norfolk, and they didn't return home until three days after everything had happened. Once they had returned, Nigel met up with them at the Blue House and made them go into hiding until the heat died down.

Chapter Four

When Scatter, Bugs, Snake, and El came towards me as I was leaving Brick Street, they told me that Prince and Beanie and strangled their boy Scoop, and although Grinch was still alive, he barely survived the gunshot wound to his stomach. Man, this shit is getting creepier by the moment; almost every day, something wild keeps happening and people are either coming up missing, or killed. "Man, you need to watch out for these creeps around here and try to stay out of this game out here in the streets cause people ain't playing with a full deck nowadays," Bugs advised. "Take it from us lil man 'cause we 'bout to cash out and move away and try to fly right, and we jetting in about two hours from now," Scatter explained. "Take care of yourself young blood, they all said in unison.

As I continued onward to the house, I started thinking about Eubie again. I just couldn't let go. Eubie and I have been friends since we were in diapers, and I just hope that he   turns up and is alright.

Soon as I reached the front end of the car that was parked in the driveway, something told me that what I was about to hear wasn't good news. Mr. Crane from down on Weston Road come to visit, its usually during the big holidays or bad news. So, I braced myself for whatever bad news I was about to hear.

Aunt Eunice looked at me with swollen and teary eyes as I walked in the living room and grabbed me and held me tight. "Eubie dead baby, Eubie dead," she cried, "And I know them bastards did it cause that boy didn't do that to himself," she added.

Mr. Crane motioned me to sit and started explaining how they found Eubie in a vacant house, and that he had been dead for at least three or four days, according to the coroner's report. He also stated that it looked as though Eubie had over-dosed on heroin and at first, they were going to rule it as a suicide, but further investigation showed signs of forced injection because of the multiple bruising all over his body, and the lab report found the heroin was tainted with a deadly substance that killed him almost instantly once he was injected.

I couldn't even cry at first 'cause I was so shocked, mad, confused, and I wanted to hit something or somebody. "Aunt Eunice held my hand and said, "I'm praying for his soul and I don't want you to hold back yo tears chile, just go in yo bedroom and have a big cry, 'cause if you don't, it's gon' eat at you for a long time." With that, I left the room and before I could close the door behind me, I slid onto the floor and broke down for what seemed like hours. Aunt Eunice finally came in and told me to get up and lie down and that she would check on me in the morning.

I don't know how I got through school during the week Eubie was found dead. I felt bad for his family, but mostly for me because I couldn't do anything to save my friend. The funeral was backed with so many folk 'cause Eubie's mom and dad had a huge family that came from all corners of the nation. His mom wanted me to give a speak, but I was so broken that she understood that I would fall to pieces at the podium; after the eulogy had begun, she fainted 'after crying loud and hard, so it really didn't matter whether I spoke or not. Everything after the funeral was a big blur to me, but I knew I had many great memories to hold onto for a lifetime, but it was gonna take a long time for me to handle this loss.

Several weeks after Eubie got killed, they found Grinch, Scatter, and this dude named Brim who was visiting from Los Angeles, tied up, gagged, and their bodies had been burnt so badly, as if they had been drenched in gasoline before being set afire, that they could not be identified for almost a week and a half. They say that three little kids discovered the bodies while playing hide and seek. People around the south end of town claim that Butchie told them that Squirm and Ed B. had done the job for a cat named Roscoe cause the word on the streets was that Brim had beat and robbed his runners Skip and Pilot down by Engine Floyd's Café three weeks ago. Brim, according to Butchie, was a huge guy that used to be a boxer growing up in LA, and he was also Scatter's cousin. He said that Scatter had told him two days before Brim made his hit on Skip and Pilot that even though he was his cousin, he didn't trust him. So, with that said, Butchie claimed that Brim lied on Grinch and said that he was responsible for what happened to Roscoe's runners, but when they caught up with him, Grinch had no idea about what was going on. Grinch and Scatter was headed down by FeFe's joint to meet some girls when they were approached by Dogg Man and Cap; they forced them into the car where Brim was already sitting and looking nervous. And then that's they took all of them and killed them.

Man, I know that I will be gone in a couple of months, but I wish it was sooner 'cause too many things have been happening. Walking pass the bridge, Old Man Carson, a homeless man who refuses to stay with his relatives 'cause he said all of them are vultures and they would bleed you dry, waved for me to join him on the bench. I knew that he was ready to lecture me about the streets, but at this point, and with all that had been going on, I figured he could tell me something beneficial to my well-being. Hey Mr. Carson, how you been doing? "Well young Blood, I been doing okay, but a lot of these young cats been getting knocked off left and right," he said. "You need to stay close to home after school and on the weekends 'cause these fools out here thirsty as hell and got all sorts of evil in their heads." "You know that boy down on River Drive got popped last night 'cause he was riding in the car with Hood and Yank, and Roscoe had his boys come down on them for forcing his niece to have sex with them, and Felix was just catching a ride with them." "I tell you son, keep your eyes opened and your ears to the streets cause these fools out here are more touched in the head than they mama's now." "Now get on cross the way and go straight home and don't stop and park your butt nowhere 'cause you know Eunice waiting on you." With that, I said good day and headed to the crib.

Chapter Five

Man, the quick long & hard lesson that I had to deal with was one of the scariest moments I've experienced on a personal note. After getting caught in what could have been something more serious, I must admit that I truly appreciate the people that care about me.

I started hanging with this dude named Brent who was also in the school's band and he played the clarinet and was also an alternate drummer for the drumline. Brent was a cool dude to hang around, or so I thought.

One day, Brent's older brother Brace, who had dropped out of school during his junior year to sale drugs for Mr. Stakes, had just been released from jail two weeks prior. Mr. Stakes' team ran the entire bottom section and a small portion of the mid-section of town, and was always at odds with many other hustlers, and Braden and a dude named Stint were his top runners until Stint set Braden up for a fall so that he could be the sole top runner.

So, Braden wanted Brent to help him set Stint up for a fall 'cause he had no one else to turn to for all the other cats on Mr. Stakes team was ordered not to deal with Braden at all or else they would disappear. I really didn't want to hear this conversation, so I told them that I was getting ready to jet to the crib, but Braden interrupted me saying, "Man, if my lil brother can help me out, I thank you should come and join us 'cause I know you got a lot of info on a lot of people, so what you gon' do?" I told him that I didn't want to have any part of this, but that whatever they planned on doing, I would keep silent about it. Braden stared me down and told me that I was a punk; I thought to myself at that moment that I would rather be a punk to him than get caught up in some bullshit.

I looked at Brent, then Braden, I told both of them that I was not coming in on this with them and then I walked away. I have witnessed too damn much in the past, and thinking about how Ms. Duby is always telling me that friends are not always friends, so, I took that thought and moved on out.

Later that night, Erb stopped by and I could over hear the conversation he was having with Aunt Eunice. My quick reaction to Braden's request had turned out to be the right one for things went real sour for the two brothers. Aunt Eunice is quite aware that she talks very loud at times, and I believe that she does this to make sure that I can hear everything that she says, but, this time, she wanted to really make herself clear, so she called out to me saying, "Dee, get yo' butt in here so you can hear what's going on!"

As I took a seat on the couch, both Aunt Eunice and Erb looked at me as if they were waiting for me to say something, but I didn't. Erb told me that if I ever decide to get involved with drugs, robbing folk, or any type of street hustle, I had him to answer to. "Listen Dee, in this game called life, there are many twists and turns, and everybody you come in contact is on some type of hustle, whether it's out in the streets, at your job, school, at home, just about everywhere," Erb explained. "But, the key is to find a hustle that is right for you and one that won't get you killed or years in jail; make sure it's beneficial to where ever you trying to go, but also remember that the game of hustling has rules, so understanding where you going, you need to understand the rues, cause can change on you in an instance and get you burnt or burn somebody close to you." "If you don't keep your ears, eyes, and mind opened to everything happening around you, the slick, sly, and the wicked gain entry and opportunity to take advantage of you, so keep your moth closed more often and always be aware of your surroundings. And although you might look at me and think I don't know nothing 'bout God, trust me, that is the only thing that I trust, cause God ain't out here in this jungle called society to do me harm or see me bring harm to myself, so that's who I trust whole-heartedly. I know folk might look at me as being some type of hypocrite, but trust me, I ain't stupid and I do know whose really in charge, regardless of the amount of mistakes I have made."

Erb made a lot of sense, and for what it's worth, I take everything that him and Aunt Eunice say to be true, 'cause I do know that although they ain't always doing the right thing, they do know better and try to teach me to do and be a better person.

Erb continued, "Dee, I need to make sure that you know that this whole street husting shit ain't no game and the only way that I thank that I can give you more proof is to show you what can happen, so, this Friday coming up, be ready to take a ride with me and my man Deacon, alright? Now, with that said, I'm out 'cause I got some things to take care of."

After Erb left, I immediately began wondering what he had in store for me and to tell you the truth, I was a bit excited and worried at the same time. Big Deac was no joke and he and Erb been running together since way before I was born; Deacon Washington was also a scary looking cat, big, brawny, and bald with a voice so thick and deep, he could out-do Barry White in one take.

Friday rolled around and after school, my nerves were shot just thinking about what Erb and Deac had in store for me. Erb and Deac were waiting for me to arrive at the house, and as soon as I had entered, they told me to get in the car. Aunt Eunice looked at me with this weird look in her eyes, and then said, "Take all of this as a real lesson that can save yo' life Dee, love you." When Aunt Eunice say she loves you, something serious is always going on, so now, I was more worried than ever.

Chapter Six

All during the ride, Erb and Deac said very little, and for the most part, all I could see was the back of their heads. Suddenly, Deac pulled over and got out of the car. Erb passed him a thick scarf and opened the back door, motioning me to get out. As I stood there, the first thing I thought was that they were going to leave me out here and I had to walk all the way back home, which was at least fifteen or twenty miles outside city limits. Looking at my surroundings, the only things I saw was an old shack on the left side of the road, then sitting far back from the road, was another old shack, but it was much larger than the one on the other side. Nothing else but dirt roads and dust was visible to me, and that's the last thing I saw before Deac tied the scarf around my head, covering my eyes. He told me that I had to be blind-folded until we reach our destination.

Man, I felt like a blind man, but since this was Erb and Deac, I wasn't too afraid of them per se, I was just concerned about where we were going and what was going to happen next. After the car came to a stop, Erb and Deac led me inside a building, then down some stairs; it was cold as ever in this joint, and I was really getting scared. All of a sudden, I heard Erb and Deac talking to another man, then they walked away, and once the sound of the footsteps died down, the man told me to take the scarf and have a seat on the cot in the corner. This place was dark, dingy-looking, and cold. There was a door with a small window with bars that had been blackened out so that no one could see in or out; the same was with the window on the other side of this small room that must lead to outside. Before he left, he told me to get comfortable and that my dinner would be coming in about an hour, and would be slid under the door from the small opening. I looked at him like he was crazy, but my mouth would not open to say nothing. What in the hell is going on, I wondered? Erb must have fell on a brick and knocked all the sense out of his head 'cause this some straight up bullshit. An hour in here might be like two or three since Erb took my watch, and made me empty my pockets, so now, I'm just stuck in this hell-hole without nothing but me and a cot; no TV, radio, nothing. These negroes are crazy.

Time seemed to drag on like the last drop of syrup in a bottle, and my stomach began to hurt and I was hungry. All I could think of at that moment was the dinner I was missing at home, 'cause Aunt Eunice always made the best meals. Just then, a rat darted in and out of sight and I really start getting freaked out.

Man, if I have to be stuck in here all night I might get bit by one of these varmints. Also, I didn't have a clue about what else might happen to crawl in here at any given moment.

When I finally decided to sit on the cot, I heard footsteps, then someone slid a huge tray, covered with aluminum foil through the slit in the bottom of the door, then a cold, grape pop; by then, I was so damn hungry, all I could do was tear into the food and drink. I don't know where this food came from, but I knew just by looking at it, Aunt Eunice hadn't cooked it, but it tasted alright nonetheless. When I had finished, I used the paper bag they had provided with the meal and placed everything inside and closed it tight 'cause I had no idea how long they were going to keep me in here and I did not want to invite any little critters to join me.

I started getting sleepy but really didn't want to go, and then I had to take a leak. Over in the corner, I found a gray pail that had a little bit of water in it, so, I took a piss in it and placed it back in the corner; if for some reason, I have to take a dump, it won't happen in here as long as I can help it.

I sat back on the cot, plumped the pillow up, then lied on my back, gazing at the ceiling; I must have dozed off to sleep because the next thing I heard was someone sliding food under the slit again. Damn, morning snuck up on me, I thought aloud. The breakfast was right on point and they even place a warm towel inside of a plastic bag for me to wash my face. Although I wasn't a big coffee drinker, I drank it and the orange juice, and after that meal, I did a few push up and running in place 'cause I had to put my mind off of my surroundings and quick. The food came on time for lunch and dinner, and then as I laid back on the cot, I became pissed all over again; I could not believe that Erb did this to me. A lesson is a lesson, but this shit was ridiculous. I was so mad again, that before I had realized it, I had fell asleep and woke up again, and this time, it had to have been Sunday morning 'cause breakfast, right on schedule. For some reason, I started to think that someone had to be checking up on me 'cause I didn't have a watch so I didn't know what time it was, and then I thought that somebody must be playing more tricks on me. I now the being in this room all of this time gave me many moments to reflect back on what had happened to Eubie and other people, and I suddenly felt that for some reason I had to be here to try and think more clearly about things.

As I was lying on the cot, lost in deep thought, I heard talking outside the door, and instantly thought that someone was coming to let me out of here. Big Benny entered the room with this crazy looking dude that look as if he would eat you alive; his name was Derk, and Benny told me that he would be my roommate from now on and that he and I had to work out the sleeping arrangements since there was only one small cot I looked at both of them in great disbelief, and all of a sudden, Derk headed towards the cot and said, "You have fun on the flo young blood, and then smiled and grinned at Big Benny."

I looked at Benny again and told him that if he thought that this shit was funny, it wasn't, and if I have to fight this man until he kills me, then so be it, but his ass was gon' get off of that cot or get knocked off. Both men started laughing so hard that it brought them to tears, but I was as serious as a heart attack, and when I started walking towards the cot, Big Benny stood in my way and shouted, "Youngblood, you really don't want to upset Derk, so I suppose you get yo' lil self over on the other side of the room and sit on that flo."

My respect for you and all of y'all, just flew out the door, so go straight to hell cause this sucker getting up off that cot, I shouted. I may be small and frail compared to Derk, but I ain't no punk, I ain't slacking down, and furthermore, as I kicked his foot, get yo' ass up.

Before anyone moved or had a chance to say anything else, Erb and Deac bust through the door laughing. I looked at all of them and bravely told them that I was leaving and if any of them got in my way, I'm fighting with all I got. They continued to find a great deal of humor in this fiasco, as if They had been watching a Richard Pryor tape. Erb finally told me to go outside and get in the car, and damn near knocked Deac down trying to get out of that hell hole.

The drive to the house took less than one minute, and once we pulled up in the driveway, Erb looked at me and said, "Now, I hope that you had time to think about all the shit that's been going on and how you can get caught up in any type of bullshit and end up in a far worse place than the one we made you stay in, cause, any other place would've been full of just about every type of crazy folk you can think of, from murderers, thieves, molesters, and you name it, anybody." On that note, I went inside of the house, took a long, hot bath, then a shower, and by the time I was back in my room, Aunt Eunice had made it home from church.

"Dee," Aunt Eunice called out after she tapped lightly on the door. She walked in with a light smile on her face and asked me if I was doing okay. I told her that I was alright. "Well, I know you felt a bit confused by all the elusiveness that went on this weekend, but listen sweetheart, we wanted you to understand what could happen to you if you don't go in with all eyes opened in all you do, so, I love you, and dinner is ready."

Since I missed lunch 'cause I was still mad about things and lunch was the last thing on my mind, I welcomed dinner with a big appetite. Boy, what a damn weekend.

Chapter Seven

Well, after spending all this time at Aunt Eunice's house, I was ready more than ever to be leaving once my mom got here. Not that I don't like being here, but with all the shenanigans that occurred with Eubie and others, I was drained and ready more than ever for a change of scenery.

Two days before Thanksgiving, my mom arrived and I was over-joyed; eighteen months seemed like ten years to me. As soon as she got here, Aunt Eunice put her to work in the kitchen; man, I can't wait until the holiday, so, I'm the official taste tester for both my mom and Aunt Eunice.

On the day of the big feast, we had relatives come for dinner that I had never seen before. These folk came from every corner of the United States. Many of the big hustlers came as well, cause a lot of them been around Aunt Eunice for a long time, and they brought their immediate families as well. Aunt Eunice has a very huge house that has nine bedrooms and 4 bedrooms, but when only she and I are here, a big part of the house is not used until family and friends come by for the holidays and for reunions; most of the people over forty stayed at the house and others got hotel rooms at one of Erb's huge hotels out in the suburbs cause they didn't have to pay for anything.

We had a ball from Thanksgiving Eve to Sunday night. On Saturday, we used one of Erb's big hall's downtown and had party night; one side was the folk over forty, and the other side was for everyone else, but midway through the evening, and after many of the over forties side got juiced up, they removed the partition and everyone partied together. The Soul Train line was hilarious cause many of the older folk brought out all the old dance moves, some were jamming, but some of them were so juiced up, they created their own dances. This was a great way to end my stay here.

Before heading for the highway, my mom and Aunt Eunice had to have their usual private talk inside her bedroom. These talks went on for at least an hour or so. I turned on the Television and started watching the weather channel to see if I can figure out what the weather would be like during the drive to Fort Bragg.

Finally, we were ready to go, so, I grabbed Aunt Eunice before she could grab me and place sloppy kisses all over my face, and was happy that Erb showed up to save me from all that sweet stuff. Erb placed a huge wad of money in my mom's hand, then came towards me, hugged me, and filled my pockets with a wad of cash. Man, I am truly gonna miss these kind of moments.

"Did you get that book and stuff I told you about, Aunt Eunice cried out to my mom. "Yes ma'am I did, love y'all to infinity," she hollered back and then we were on the road. Soon as I got seated just right, I popped my cassette in and relaxed. Here we come North Click……

North Carolina wasn't that bad, from what I gathered; the weather was a bit warmer than back home in Akron, Ohio. I decided to check my cash and to my surprise, I had over seven hundred dollars in twenties. Erb was my kind of dude. My mom looked at me and said, "Don't get no high ideas about spending that money too fast cause you need to start a savings account." "So, how much of the cash are you going to start your account off with?" she asked. I wanted to say none or at least twenty dollars, but I knew that wouldn't go over good with her, so, I told her that I thought about depositing five hundred of it, and she agreed.

We got a real nice house on base, and for my mom, she was even more happy about being closer to the officers' housing area and away from most of the lower enlisted. She was a sergeant first class by now and she had a great position where she worked as an instructor, so for at least the next two or three years, she would be locked in to it, unless she extends, and this means that I should be able to graduate from the high school here.

Just when I thought things were going to be a little boring, I finally found another individual that I could hang out with that I didn't have to keep watching my back over and over. Sa Evans was a cool dude, and we were both were sophomores, (I had been advanced to tenth grade once I got here due to the advanced courses I took in Ohio). His dad and mom were Master Sergeants and they had arrived two days before me and my mom did. We both joined JROTC, and the band; Sa played saxophone and guitar, and was also on the drumline which was his main position in the band. Sa also had two younger brothers and a sister; his sister Kema was a freshmen and his twin brothers, Donovan and Jonathan were in middle school, in the seventh grade. Sa and I fought plenty of guys after school over his sister Kema cause although she was only a freshman, the older guys, especially those on the football and basketball teams, would try getting with her, and she made it even worse by egging them on. But one day, I looked at Sa and told him that if things keep going the way that they have been, we might end up getting the worse end of the stick, and even though we were thinking about slacking off a bit, Kema had already made up her mind to become sneakier and started dating this senior named Bryan Ambrose.

Before summer hit, she found herself pregnant and without a boyfriend, cause homeboy had a scholarship to play ball at Notre Dame, and he stopped communicating with her. Come to find out, his scholarship was not at Notre Dame, it was Purdue, and the baby was not his, it was his dad's, Sergeant First Class Vincent Ambrose. Ambrose was a part of my mom's unit but he worked at battalion as head of personnel for headquarters. One of the other sergeant's in my mom's building was a so an instructor and she was Bryan's mother's best friends, but this woman told everything to my mom, now that's what some best friends do to their so-called best friends, share your personal business with others; this is some of the stuff that Aunt Eunice and my mom used to talk to me about all the time cause they said that people use the term "Friend" too loosely, and that I need to have as less friends as possible.

Ambrose's wife caught him and Kema in their bedroom. She freaked out and ran out of the house and was so upset when she got into her car that she did not see the van behind her as she slammed on the gas and crashed into it. Fortunately, the guy in the van was drunk as ever, and for some reason, the MPs blamed him for the wreck, so she got off scott-free and only had a big not on her forehead from the event. To make a long story short, Ambrose was kicked out of the Army, but since Kema's parents really didn't want to drag all this mess in the public, they didn't file charges against him, so, the battalion commander also stripped him of his rank and put him out at the rank of specialist; what an embarrassment.

Unfortunately for Kema, her baby was stillborn, and she had to spend a few months in a mental institution, and after she was released, her parents sent her to Alabama to stay with her grandparents until she graduates high school.

Chapter Eight

When my mom made master sergeant, her unit gave her a dinner at this fancy restaurant and everyone brought their families. I met a lot of the military brats that lived off-base and attended other high schools. Me and Sa got a lot of girls' phone numbers that day.

Everything seemed to be going well until one day, my mom came home crying, saying that we needed to pack a few cloths quickly cause we were getting ready to catch a flight to Ohio. The first thing that came to mind was that somebody had died, but she told me that Aunt Eunice was very ill and was taken to the hospital but they think that she would be alright. In my mind and gut, I had the feeling that there was a lot more to this story than we knew about. I figured that if Aunt Eunice's condition was worse than they claimed, they decided to not say so 'cause they know my mom would panic. I just couldn't shake this feeling.

Once we got to the hospital, Erb met us as soon as we got out of the car; he had sent Deac to pick us up from the airport. While Erb tried to comfort my mom before we got to the room, I looked at Deac and I think he understood what I was trying convey to him, 'cause he gave me this nod that said it all then he kind of shifted his eyes to the floor. I braced myself for the real news.

As we entered the room, Aunt Eunice called out my mom's name before anyone even said anything. "I always know when you come into a room without even looking 'cause I can smell that lotion you always wearing," she said, in a very weak voice. She was slowly drifting away, but for a brief moment, she gained enough strength to whisper something in my mom's ear, but a soon as she was finished, I heard her say I love all of you and don't forget none of my life lessons and scoldings.... then she gently closed her eyes, took her last breath, and once my mom closed her eyes, she just laid there, looking as if she was asleep.

We all stood round her bed until they came to get her, just standing, and silently crying. Erb finally spoke and said, "Well, she is on her way to a long, long slumber and I pray that God saves her soul." I looked at him, puzzled by what he had just said, 'cause although I know Aunt Eunice would cuss every now and again, I did know that she was deep off into her church; so, what was Erb talking about, I wondered.

The funeral for Aunt Eunice was very sad; there were so many people there, and many of them I had no idea if they were relatives or not, but just about everyone were crying hard. My mom had been crying so much prior to the funeral that she was more calm than most folk, and she sang two of Aunt Eunice's favorite songs. Although she kept it together during the funeral, my mom lost it at the cemetery.

We stayed in Ohio for three days after the funeral 'cause my mom had to take care all of Aunt Eunice's businesses; she owned several houses, apartment buildings, the two car lots and three liquor stores that I thought was owned by Erb, and two cars, plus this house. Everything went to my mom, but, since she put Erb down as general manager and her cousin Stymie oversees all of the other businesses, but she held on to the deeds of all of it, and the main house and two cars, (a brand new Cadillac and a vintage jaguar), she placed in storage. Well, Aunt Eunice also had another secret diary for my mother to open after her death, but my mom wanted to wait until we return to North Carolina before she viewed it. Although Aunt Eunice left the Jag to my mom, she also had a note in her will that once I complete college, the Jag was mine.

Once we had returned to NC, my mom read the secret diary, but for some reason, she did not share its content with me. I was a bit taken aback by her not wanting to share because we are very close, but, I decided that whatever was inside that diary had to be a real doozy, but that she would eventually let me know what was in there.

Chapter Nine

By the time my senior year in high had rolled around, I had decided that I wanted to go into the military instead of going to college, but, my mom had a real issue with that. She told me that since I had a couple of years under my belt in JROTC, why not enroll in a college that offered ROTC and then enter the military as an officer? I had to really think long and hard about that one, cause, my dudes Sa, Denchie, and Carl were all ready to enlist in the Army, and I wanted to do the same. Besides, I already had college credit from being dual-enrolled in high school and college at the same time; I had completed English comp one and two, college algebra and physics, and four other courses, so I already had about thirty credits, and I could also test out of a few more courses before enlisting or once I enlist.

Well, it turned out that my mom finally agreed that going into the Army would be good for me, so when I told her that I was thinking about the supply field, she thought it was a good idea. So, 3 months prior to graduation, I enlisted for four years as a supply specialist and since I already had college credit, I get to go in as a private first class. Dench and Carl copied another one of our classmates, Wynton, and enlisted as infantry soldiers, and Sa decided to enlist as a warehouse supply specialist, Me and Sa couldn't believe those guys were gonna be in the infantry field, but they were looking at the big bonuses they would receive; they had to enlist for six years though.

The first two years in the Army went by so fast, that I almost forgot about taking my last course so that I could receive my BA in business management. My mom instantly suggested that I put in for OCS once I shared the news of getting my BA with her, and I kind of agreed that it was time. I was made a corporal last week when I had replaced the Armorer, but although many folks wouldn't want this job, it suited me fine. Two days after talking with my mom, our battalion got orders for Beirut, and when I told my mom, she responded, "Well, the choice is up to you 'cause your dad didn't have any other kids, and by you being an only son, you really don't have to go, but the choice is yours, whatcha gonna do?" I decided that I was a real soldier, and I was going although I knew my mom wasn't too thrilled about it, but she understood cause she had gone to places similar to this as well.

After being in our destination for about two weeks, I ran in Sa; his unit was attached to one of our supply company in the battalion. He told me that Denchie's sister, Katina had written and told him that he and a few of his soldiers got bombed, and that he didn't make it. This was sad news and I prayed for his family, but I told Sa that if he and Carl would have followed in our footsteps and came into the supply field, this wouldn't have happened, but Sa looked up and we both realized, without speaking that this and more could happen to anyone regardless of their MOS, even us.

As the New Year rang in, I realized that we had been here for almost two years without losing anyone, but, I had a gut feeling that things were about to get serious. Well, just like my gut feeling always warn me, something major occurred and it left me kind of down in the dumps for at least two months. We were out on a mission filling sandbags when we got hit. My squad freaked out, but knowing that I had to hold it together in order for us to survive, I took my fear and tucked it inside and rolled on. When two of my soldiers got trapped under a five ton that had been hit, I couldn't leave 'em, so I managed to go above and beyond and found strength that I never knew I had. Me and the other soldiers freed one of the men, but it was very difficult to reach the other one, so, I ordered everybody to take cover and I stayed back to get my man out. After some quick praying and maneuvering, I got him out, straddled him across my back and low-crawled to the nearest safe spot, and waited for about thirty minutes, then high-tailed it out of there with my soldier on my back, my weapon and gear tight and secure, and didn't look back.

When we got to another unit in our battalion's camp, several soldiers rushed to help me get the injured soldier inside; I fell to the ground and hid my face inside of my hands and thanked God for getting us to safety.   The soldier, private Bradley, sustained a gunshot wound to his right leg, and a few gashes on both arms, but, after being down for about a week and a half, he pulled through.   They told me that I had gotten him free just in time before his ribs got crushed, and if we had gotten hit while being near the vehicle, he wouldn't have made it out.   I received several awards for what I looked at as just simply doing my job as a leader, but for many folk, it was a huge deal.

Things were heating up over there, and about three months after the previous incident, another painful event occurred.   One of the soldiers from another squad had received some bad news from home, and the commander immediately placed him on suicide watch. When it came time for rotation, two of my soldiers had to relieve the other soldiers and their watch consisted of two hours each.   The soldier had been falling deeper and deeper into depression and I decided to check up on my soldiers that were standing watch, and it's a good thing I did.   When I looked in on Bradley, at first glance, he appeared to had been sleeping, but something drove me closer; his face looked funny, so I touched his right jaw, and it was cold as ice.

I was as calm as I could be and figured that maybe he just need more cover, but as I checked for a pulse, I couldn't find one in his neck or his wrist. Without panicking, I told one of my soldiers to call for help. As we were waiting for the platoon sergeant, who also told me to call the MPs to arrive, I questioned my soldiers and they informed me that they had just relived the previous guards no longer forty minutes ago, and they reported that all was well and that Bradley had just fell off to sleep.

Once Bloom and the MPs arrived, it was instantly stated by the MPs that an investigation will be happening in the morning. I believed my soldiers when they explained that they had not engaged in any wrong doing, but this whole thing looked fishy.

The soldiers that had relieved my soldiers tried to say that they must have slipped something to Bradley because he was only sleeping when they were leaving. Come to find out, these two soldiers had had it in for Bradley because he made private first class before either of them did, and they didn't like him from the first day he came to the unit. Private Jackson was the ring leader, but private Rutherford couldn't hold water if it splashed down on him in bed, and he made the mistake of saying that he didn't realize that the pain pills he was given from the doctor last week when he went on sick call for an injury he got was as powerful as they were; coincidentally, the lab report on Bradley tested positive for codeine, and Bradley had not been on sick call since we arrived here.

Jackson threatened to lie on Rutherford if he didn't give him the pills and help him get rid of Bradley. One thing that appeared odd and eventually made this case easier to solve, was that these two had paid previous guards to let them take their place, so they had a total of six hours to make sure that things went the way that Jackson wanted them to. The rotation was so out of order that Jackson and Rutherford's duty shouldn't have occurred until after my two soldiers' post.

Rutherford got Jackson to help him hold Bradley down, then he forced the pills down his throat five pills at a time and gave him water in between each take. Jackson said that it looked as if Bradley didn't even want to fight and was willing to take the pills cause he was ready to die. This was crazy, but true, and just looking at how people, especially those who are Black like you, can be so cruel and evil. Unfortunately, as I suspected when I touched Bradley's face, he was dead. Rutherford and Jackson were dishonorably discharged, and were sentenced to twenty-five to life.

After almost three years, we finally returned to the states and I had been promoted to sergeant and I was also promotable to staff sergeant. I was so thrilled to be back in the states, and finally able to move out of the barracks and get my own crib. While I was apartment hunting, I met this chick named Joi; she was fine as ever. Joi and I started dating, more often once I had found an apartment that I shared with staff sergeant Leon Grayson. We had a three-bedroom apartment that was about a ten-minute drive from base. Joi was a practical nurse at the hospital on base. Leon was seeing at least four females at the same time, but it could be more. Leon was a bit of a player, but, he was a cool dude and we got along just fine.

Joi was friends with Wanda, one of the ladies that Leon had been seeing more of and she was ready to get married. Wanda was a staff sergeant like Joi, but she worked as a trauma nurse. I thought that out of all of the ladies, Wanda was a good fit for Leon, but he was more into Daphne. Daphne was a hustler. She was stripping down at one of the joints downtown, and for the life of me, I couldn't see how he was stuck on this woman, but that was his thang, not mine. Although Daphne was a stripper, she wasn't that bad of a person; she was trying to take care of her four-year-old daughter, and attending grad school during the day. The other two heifers, Sophia and Eadie were a totally different breed of females. They both were fine looking, light skinned, shoulder length hair, but had egos bigger than Europe. Sophia was a military brat whose dad is a retired full bird, and she is spoiled to the core and has a rotten attitude. Eadie, is the sister of a military officer, who by the way, is her third husband, and Eadie has been on a serious hunt to snatch up a husband sense she became an adult. Eadie is the type of woman that is too damn friendly, and from what many folks say, she has been sleeping around with half of the base. Leon is playing with fire, in my opinion, and whomever he ends up with, somebody's gonna get burnt............

Chapter Ten

Joi and I had been getting pretty close, but, for some reason, I had my doubts about the future for us. For one thing, I got a gut feeling that Joi has not been as truthful with me about her past relationships. For starters, when her mom came down to visit her, she brought along a little girl that Joi had called her niece, but, I discovered that Joi only has one sibling, and he is gay, and as far as I know, has never been with a woman, but she has never shared with me how this little girl is her niece. The little girl's name is Princess Joi and she is seven years-old and favors Joi an awful lot.

One day, while Mrs. Johnson and Princess came by for dinner, I overheard Joi fussing at Princess in the bathroom when I was on my way to the bedroom to get something. Once I had reached the bedroom, I heard Princess say, "But mommy, I didn't say nothing for him to hear," and then I heard Joi mumbling something and Princess started crying a little louder so I went to the door and asked what was going on. Joi quickly told me that things were fine, but as I looked at Princess, I could see that her left cheek was a little red.

I told Princess to go into the living room so that I could speak with Joi in private, but Joi snatch Princess and rushed her into the living room before I could say more. This was getting stranger by the minute, and somebody was gonna tell me something before leaving my house tonight.

I entered the living room and asked what was going on, and Joi snapped at me saying, "Nothing that I don't have control of, so don't worry about it." I asked the same question, one more time, and all of a sudden, Joi jumped up and told her mom that it was time for them to be leaving. Her mom looked at me, and I went to the door and blocked it, and I told Princess to go to my room and close the door, but Joi tried to stop her, then I grabbed Joi, and motioned Princess to go. Mrs. Johnson stood up shouting, "What the hell is going on Joi?"

I looked at her and said that was exactly what I wanted to know. Joi didn't say a word. Why do Princess have a red mark on her face, did you slap her? Mrs. Johnson's mouth dropped wide open, and she walked towards Joi and asked her if she had hit Princess, and she denied it so Mrs. Johnson went to the bedroom to talk to Princess. I looked at Joi and asked her again, in a very low voice, and she still denied it.

Once her mom had returned from the room, she slapped Joi so hard, I felt like she had slapped me.

"You hurt this baby again, and I told you that if you ever put your hands on her again, I'd kill you with my bare hands," she growled. Let me tell you something Dee, this bitch lost custody of Princess when she was two because she started abusing her when her husband started cheating on her," she offered. This was new to me because Joi told me that she had never been married before and she didn't have any kids. Mrs. Johnson said that two years ago, Joi's husband got station in Korea and she hadn't heard from him since, and Joi lost permanent custody of Princess soon after that. All while her mom was talking, Joi looked out of the window, as if no one else was in the room. Mrs. Johnson also told me that Joi has to take medication for her anger issues that she's had since she was seven, and that she becomes out of control with her anger when things don't go her way.

I was so done; how long did this heifer think she could hide all of this from me. Well, so much for that relationship going any further. Mrs. Johnson apologized to me, and told me that I need to leave her daughter alone because she won't be any good for no one until she gets some help for herself and find that damn husband of hers and get a divorce.

I couldn't believe this night, but, evidently, it was meant to happen in order for me to see what was really going on. I just pray that this woman gets some help before she destroys herself or somebody else, and I thank God that her mom has sole custody of her daughter.

Talk about crazy women, I hadn't heard from Sa in about two years when he showed up at my job one day. He, like myself, had finally made sergeant first class and he was stationed at Fort Meade MD and I was down in Norfolk, working in a Navy Logistics Unit. I also heard that Leon, my former roommate, was also stationed at Fort Meade.

Sa claimed that Leon had married Daphne, and she kept sleeping around on him and had at least four abortions, then she got him so deep in debt, that by the time he found out that she had also been sleeping with his commander and the battalion's sergeant major, they gave him a medical discharge for having several nervous breakdowns, and now, he's back in his hometown of Philly, remarried and got a daughter and a son. And of all people, he ended up with Wanda, because she was from Pittsburg, and they had run into one another while they both were at the VA hospital. "So, in the end, Wanda was the right woman for Leon, he just got all caught up in the vanity and deception of Daphne," Sa stated. Sa also said that the last he heard of Daphne, she hooked up with this white guy who got her hooked on drugs, and then dumped her, and her sister is raising her daughter now because they haven't seen Daphne in a long time.

Chapter Eleven

Sa was doing good for himself these days, he had finally settled down and had three kids, so now, it was my turn. I guess by me growing up around the people that I did, I value my kinfolk's words of wisdom more than I had realized, therefore, I had become too picky for my own good. I finally decided that it was time for me to find a wife and have a few youngins' of my own.

Sa still looked the same, and our friendship was still good, and later after working hours, he stopped by my crib and we continued getting each updated about things.

Man Sa, me and my mom's had to go home to Ohio to straighten out some business, and man, so many things had happened before I got there and while I was there. It is almost like shit be going on all day, every day, and people coming up iced and turned out on drugs by the dozens. Big Stuff told me that Rizz and Bond iced K-Dogg for his part in raping Bond's cousin Phoebe, and they found Pooky Lane's sister Margie and her friend Geneva's bodies in Kensington's Pool Hall in one of the back storage rooms in a big freezer, wrapped in heavy furniture plastic, badly beaten, strangled and both of them had plungers stuck inside of their you-know-what. First thing on the streets was that Burns and Avery had done the deed for Ink cause both girls were hooking for him and everyone knew how much he abused his women. The sad thing about all of this is that Margie was only seventeen and Geneva was fifteen. Ink got capped as he was getting out of his car early one morning; they shot him in the back of his head and left his body in the driveway. Once they caught up with Bond's body burned up and his head was detached down on Peadway Avenue, but they said that Rizz was on the run. Ms. Duby, however, went to Pooky and Stance and told them that this shit didn't have nothing to do with Ink, 'cause she saw Mordechai Weiss and three other White men scoop them girls up, and you know Ms. Duby see everything and she wouldn't lie.

Come to find out, Judge Henry Weiss, who was Mort's older brother, whose entire family was supposedly connected to a mob-type operation, was getting back at Ink for killing his daughter Natalie and beating the rap; everybody knew that her death had Ink written all over it, even in the Black community, cause this was only one way that he got rid of women he was done with 'cause they were either trying to leave his fold or because they were holding money back from him. Natalie's little brother found her body in her bedroom, and she had O.d.'d on heroin. The weird thing about her death is that she went missing for over two years 'cause Ink had placed her and a few other females in one of his houses out in Reno, Nevada to keep Judge Weiss from finding her, but once he brought the women back to Ohio, he had learned that she had tried to break away from the fold with about thirty grand, and was ratted out by Cynt and Mae, so, Ink personally gave her tainted Heroin and had Beater an Marv break into the Weiss's home and place her dead body in her bed. So, for this, Judge Weiss had to get Ink back. Nobody has heard from Rizz, but Mae, and she ain't talking to no one about his whereabouts.

Sa shook his head and said, "Man, nothing's change back home where I'm from either, cause so much killing, robbing, and deaths have been happening on a daily basis as well, and when it hits your own family, it's even more crazy." My cousin Angus was found shot and bludgeoned to death in his girlfriend's basement, and come to find out, she and her brother did it.

Well, so much for news from home man, how is your wife and kids doing? Well, my son Marco is two now, and my daughter, Brittney is four and getting ready to start school," he offered. "So, when are you going to get hitched and have some little Dees running around?" he asked, laughingly.

86

Man Sa, I have the slightest idea 'cause a lot of these women out here ain't right and they on a serious hustle to get a husband and have babies for the wrong reasons, but, that doesn't mean that I'm not still looking. In fact, I ran into an old friend from Fort Gordon one day; Reena was still as gorgeous as she was back when we first met. The last time I saw her, I was TDY at Fort Gordon for three months; she was a communications soldier in the headquarters office, in charge of operations, and we hit it off quite well.

But before I get into that story, let me tell you about this one chick I was shacking up with for almost two years; you ain't gonna believe the shit that I went through with her. She came from a family that was crazy as hell, and most of the women were so damn snobbish, it didn't make sense. Her name was Alyssa Stone, and she was from Kentucky. Her dad was a retired captain, but he was already married when her mom met him. Her mom, Betty, almost ruined this man's marriage and career. So, let me back up and start from the beginning though. I met this girl at the mall in San Francisco, and back then, I ran with this group of guys that played in a night club on the weekends, and since I played sax and they needed a new player since their guy Rome had PCS'd, I joined them and it turned out, that while talking to Alyssa, she and her cousin Vanessa were attending college out there, but, they sang back up for this band almost every night, and every weekend to make extra money. So, she and agreed to come sit in and listen to me and my boys one Friday.

When that Friday rolled around, me and the guys had about thirty minutes before we hit the stage, so we were just chilling when Alyssa and her cousin Vanessa stopped by. As soon as Irvin spotted Vanessa, I think that dude fell in love on the spot. Irvin said, man Dee, why you didn't tell me that Alyssa had such a gorgeous cousin?" I could instantly fill a little tension coming from Alyssa 'cause, truthfully, Vanessa was better looking and had a better body than she did, but I broke the ice and just laughed it off and asked the women if they wanted to sing one or two songs during our set, and at first, Alyssa was a bit reluctant, but Vanessa was all in. Something told me at that moment that Alyssa was jealous of her cousin, and that Vanessa probably song better than her; and I was right. Both ladies sound good, but Vanessa's voice was so good, I could have sworn that she was a professional that had been doing this thang for a long time.

Once the set was over, and I decided to give Alyssa a ride, cause Vanessa and Irvin had already left together, so, we headed for this all-night restaurant about two blocks from the club. Once we got there, I could tell that Alyssa had something on her mind that was obviously bugging her, so I asked her what was going in with her. "Well, for one thing, I can't stand my cousin sometimes 'cause she always trying to show off and thinks that she can sing better than me and everything else," she snapped. I let her get everything off her chest and finally, I had heard enough.

Listen Alyssa, I told her, both of you have an amazing talent, and it really doesn't matter who people think is the best singer, it's actually about how the talent is used to deliver a song to make people feel it, I told her. But she wouldn't let it go, and said, "It ain't just about the singing and tonight, she always trying to outdo me and she always get people to believe that she's better than me, and this has been going on since we were in high school," she explained. Before I could interrupt and tell her that all of this didn't matter to me, she continued to rant. She told me that her mom said that Vanessa's mom came from the ghetto and before she had met and married her brother Jacob, she was nothing and had no type of good up-bringing and more than likely got pregnant with Vanessa to move out of her dreadful surroundings. I found out later that Vanessa's mom had a beautiful voice as well, and although her family didn't have a lot of money and fancy houses and cars, they were well respected and had eventually moved out of projects and in to a decent neighborhood. Also, Vanessa graduated two years early from high school, which makes her two years younger than Alyssa, but Alyssa failed to tell me that she flunked most of her sophomore classes and had to repeat this grade as well as attend summer school.

I also found out that the real reason Alyssa was able to finally graduate high school, was because she had been sleeping with her counselor, who was a woman, and her basketball coach, who was a man. She also blackmailed her Math teacher after she walked in on him and a fellow male student getting it on in his classroom's closet.

Anyway, back to where me and Alyssa getting closer. After that night, listening to Alyssa go on and on about her cousin, I finally told her that it had been a long day, so, I called it a night. I didn't hear from her for about a month and a half 'cause for one thing, I could see drama coming, and I really didn't have time to be dealing with another disturbed female.

Irving had become more and more serious about Vanessa, so, they finally decided to get married. He asked all of us in the band, which was me, Micky Ro, Jeff Allen, George Frierson, and Juan Ramos. Although each of us tried to get Irvin to slow down and wait a few more months, he was dead set on getting married to Vanessa, and nothing or no one was going to talk him out of it. Vanessa was a good woman, but all of this just seemed to happen to fast, but Irvin insisted that he had found his woman for life; it turned being the truth 'cause they are still together.

I asked Vanessa one day, as the wedding date was getting closer, if she had heard from her cousin Alyssa and if so, was she planning on inviting her to the wedding. She answered, "If I had my way, me and Irvin would be headed to Vegas, but, my dad wants all of his side of the family to come, and I am so dreading it, and I am unsure about what's been going on with Alyssa 'cause I haven't heard from her in a long while, and she even stopped singing in our group." "I guess she will make her presence known at the wedding," she added.

Two weeks before the wedding, I stopped by to see Irvin at his house, and Alyssa was there, looking good I might add. "Well, hello Dee, how are you doing?" she smilingly said. I'm doing good, and you? "I'm doing good, and especially since I finally got my BA, now I need a job." Alyssa had graduated a few weeks ago, and oddly, Vanessa didn't mention this event because she had graduated with high honors two months ago; this was yet another blow to Alyssa's ego, so maybe this is why Vanessa hadn't mentioned it to me.

As I was preparing to sit down, Alyssa asked me to join her in the dining room to talk for a bit, so, I agreed. "I really want to get on a better foot with you Dee 'cause I had the feeling that I rubbed you the wrong way, especially by ranting about something as frivolous as it was, and I really don't want you to think of me in that way, so, can we start anew?" she asked. My gut said run, but, I decided to give her another chance. We ended the day at my crib, and by the time the wedding day had arrived, we had been seeing one another every day. She really impressed me with the big change in everything, but my mom's and Aunt Eunice's voices stayed boldly in my head. Aunt Eunice would tell me to never mistake a penny for a dime 'cause looks can be deceiving and the regrets will lay heavy in your way for a very long time; my mom would tell me to stop looking at asses and listen to the words coming out of their mouths and watch their actions and how they talk and act around everyone they happen to come in contact with while you are with them. But, I was not taking heed and felt that as a man who was doing quite well in my job and everything, single and ready to settle down, I had to make my own decisions. Boy, do I ever wish I would have paid closer attention to what they were telling me.

Chapter Twelve

Once Vanessa's family and friends started rolling into town, things became real interesting. I met a lot of folk that was nuttier than a fruitcake, but some of them were alright, mostly on Vanessa's mom's side of the tree. Her dad's and Alyssa's folk had a lot of issues and some of these folk's nose was so far up their asses that the entire time they were in town, I started thinking I was at a live Broadway play, cause so many of them on Alyssa's side was working hard to keep a lot of the family secrets from being revealed, especially once Alyssa's uncle MoBo on her mom's side got all juiced up and started blabbing on a lot of his own sisters' business, and there were a total of seven sisters and three brother in that family. I mean Sa man, these folk were so damn stuck up and tried their best to upstage Vanessa's side of the family, but, many of them came ready to battle, some wanted to get physical, but, unlike what Alyssa led me to believe, Vanessa's mom's side of the tree had a few interesting folks that had big money 'cause a couple of them were doctors, lawyers, and many of her cousin had college degrees and good jobs.

Vanessa had a gorgeous sister named Pearlie and she was one year younger than I was, single, one daughter. She was also a corporate lawyer for a huge business, and I almost wanted to forget Alyssa and get with Pearlie, but it turned out that she basically fit in good with Alyssa's mom's side and they accepted her 'cause she was just as stuck up as they were. In fact, I learned from their uncle MoBo that Pearlie had gotten Alyssa's brother Orbie's son Braden off after he was jailed for drug possession, robbery and a few other things; Pearlie had a few connections, so, she hooked him up. So, ever since then, that side of the tree been kissing up to her, but they still talk trash behind her back.

Well, everything went as better than everyone had expected and the newlyweds were on their way to Paris for a week, but a few of the folk stayed over for a few more days, including Alyssa's mom and her sister Mariah. Alyssa's uncle MoBo wanted to go buy some liquor, so, he asked me to take him; Alyssa wanted to tag along, but her mom wanted her to do something with her hair, so me and MoBo left. After being gone away from the others, I saw why they didn't want him to be left alone with me, 'cause for one, he spilled the beans about a few people in his family to me. He told me that Mariah had been married before and had twins, a boy and a girl, but they were being raised by their dad. Mariah's ex was a retired Naval officer with thirty-five years under his belt, but the real reason that she was divorced was because she was gay and her mom forced her to marry Frank, who was also a formal ensign under their dad's command years ago, and Frank was fifteen years older than Mariah. Her other sister Terri had five kids, and her aunt Mabel was raising the first three, and the other two were with their dads. Mariah's ex-husband, Noel caught her in the bed with his youngest sister; it turns out that while the girl had been visiting them one summer and used as a babysitter, and Mariah had used that opportunity to turn the young lady out. Noel got fed up and this was the last straw because he had already caught her with two of his soldier's wives, and one of the women's husband left her and their four kids, and one other soldier and his wife wanted to turn Mariah in for turning out their thirteen-year-old daughter, but decided to squash it because they didn't want others to find out about their business. So, Noel decided that he had had enough of Mariah's mess and this was the last time that she would be doing it as his wife. She didn't want the kids, and frankly, Noel wasn't going to let her have them anyway.

Now, Terri was another confused and messed up woman, she had married a guy in the military that couldn't have kids, but not until he kept catching messing around on him did he learn that none of the kids were his, and all of them had different fathers; two of the kids were by one of his section chiefs, but he never confronted him, and he gathered up the kids and Terri and drove for fifteen hours one weekend and left them at her mom's house in Kentucky. No one has ever heard from him since. MoBo looked at me while we were waiting for the light to turn green and he said, "Boy, you better walk in this thang with yo' eyes wide open cause all them Bitches crazy cause they got it from they mama and grandma and further back than that." And further mo,' I don't come around nine of 'em cause they know I will talk shit and don't care who gets mad about it, so you need to thank long and hard 'bout fooling with these women.

Once we got back to the hotel where Alyssa and her mom was, everybody stared at me and MoBo like we had stolen something. I suppose they were scared that MoBo been talking too much, which he had, but I wasn't going to tell them what he had said. "It took y'all long enough, where did you go, to England," Alyssa said sarcastically. I didn't respond, but MoBo offered, "Aw hush up lil gal, we went where we went and that' that!" Alyssa rolled her eyes so hard I thought she was gonna cut him if she blinked them, and her mom just looked like she had an empty, cold, and blank face, so, with all that tension building up, I thought to myself that it was time for me to exit. I wished them all a safe trip back home and I jetted before Alyssa could ask me anything, but she did manage to ask me to call her later.

I kept my dealings with Alyssa to a bare minimum, cause I didn't want to get too attached, and I definitely didn't want her to get too close to me either, but it was too late; home girl was getting too close, regardless of how I tried to limit our seeing each other.

When I told her that I had orders for Japan, she started crying and told me that she had just found out that she was two months pregnant with twins. I looked at her in shock. I could not believe this shit was happening. I had never meant to get caught up in some shit like this. She looked at me and asked what was I planning on doing about it, and I simply told her that I had to take a moment and think about everything, and she got up and started throwing shit around my living room, and I grabbed her arm and asked her what the hell was wrong with her, and she plopped down on the bed and kept crying, but now that I look back on that dramatic moment, I don't remember seeing nam damn tear, but I was still shocked at what she had told me.

I walked into the kitchen shaking my head, and as soon as I turned around, she through a piece of paper at me then turned around and walked out the door, slamming it so hard, one of the pictures on my wall fell down. When I looked at the paper, it was from a clinic showing a positive pregnancy test, then I saw her name, and then, hit the wall so hard, I thought that I had left a hole in it. I folded the paper, and later, I placed it inside the pockets of a book cover, and left it there, never looking at it again until years later.

So, two days had gone by and I hadn't seen or heard from Alyssa, so, I went by her apartment, and the man in the apartment across from hers told me that she flew to Kentucky and was going to be gone for a couple of weeks cause she wanted my girlfriend to get her mail for her. Since it was Thursday, I decided to put in for a five-day weekend so that I could catch a flight to Kentucky to see what was going on, cause I didn't want this girl to do something stupid like get rid of my child and make me look as if I was irresponsible, so I was preparing to jet out of here.

I rented a car after I had landed, and went straight to Alyssa's mom's house. Before I could get out of the car, her mom came rushing over to the car and asked me what did I plan on doing about her daughter and the baby. I spoke to her then asked where Alyssa was, and she shouted, "You didn't answer my question yet" I looked at her then boldly explained to her that whatever my decision was going to be, me and Alyssa would be discussing it alone. At that moment, I could have sworn she had steam coming out of her eyes, cause she gave me this hard look as if she wanted to attack me, but I just asked her again about Alyssa's whereabouts, so she snapped back with attitude and said, "She's in the house, you can come on in." I really didn't want to come into her home, 'cause I could already see that it was about to be a whole lot of shit coming.

Alyssa told me that he had scheduled an abortion for the upcoming Monday, and I told her that she wasn't going to kill no baby of mine, so, we needed to make wedding plans real soon. I decided that if I was going to be a daddy, I may as well do it right and be a husband as well 'cause that was the kind of man my mom's raised, and besides, I never got the chance to know my dad because he was killed when I was almost two. But, I hadn't told my mom about my plans, I know that she is gonna be highly pissed.

All of a sudden, Alyssa's mom started acting like the perfect mother in-law, and even her sisters and other relatives started treating me like I was a king; MoBo pulled me to the side before Alyssa's mom came near us, and said, "Boy, you fucking up, 'cause these bitches are crazy, and if you think that life is going to be all honkey dory, you need your head checked, but, since you already made your mind up, I hope you keep your eyes opened, 'cause you about to see some things that you never thought was coming."   At this point, it didn't matter to me 'cause I knew what I had to do.

The only person I was concerned about talking to was my mom.

Once I returned to the crib, I was on my way to the bathroom and the phone rang. It was my mom. "Boy, what the hell is going on, I know something ain't right 'cause I have been feeling oddly all week, what's going on," she asked. When I told her about Alyssa being pregnant and that I had planned on marrying her 'cause I had just received orders for Japan, she didn't say anything for at least two minutes, and I knew she was pissed. "Well, she finally said, you stepped in this pile of shit, now you got to smell it." "Now, how in the hell did you figure on this being your child for one," she scolded. "For all you know, this heifer may be pregnant by someone else or better yet, she may have forged the document just to get you to marry her." "You know damn well these types of women are always on a hustle to trap somebody, and your butt got too much sense to be getting caught up like this." I didn't' say shit, because if I did, I would have to hear more shit than I was willing to, so I let her talk. "So, when is the wedding," she asked. I told her that we would probably get married within the next two weeks 'cause I have to be in Japan in less than two months, and I wanted to take leave before going over. Although she was disappointed in my decision, my mom simply let it go, and told me that she loved me no matter what, but, to be careful 'cause she felt a heavy storm brewing.

As soon as Alyssa and I were trying to plan for the big day, it seemed as if all kinds of obstacles were blocking the flow of things, and the biggest one was my increased duties at work. My position was a serious one, and while I tried to train my successor, his lack of knowledge and skills became far too evident, so, my commander called me in to his office one day. "Robinson, we got a serious situation on hand," he said. "Now, I realize that you are preparing to go on leave before heading to Japan, but, we might have to cut your leave in half until we can replace Marsh because this NCO just don.t match up to what we need in this unit, therefore, I need you to comply with this decision?" I wanted to tell him no, but the soldier in me agreed to only take two weeks instead of an entire month of leave.

When I discussed things with Alyssa, she became upset, and told me that I needed to hurry and get things settled so that I can go to Japan. I looked at her as if she was a stranger because the first thing that came to my mind is that she should be trying to plan a wedding and then hurry and get her passport and prepare to leave with me, but I learned that she hadn't even applied for it yet; the excuse she gave me for not wanting to get things going so that we could leave for Japan together, or for her to come later before she got too far gone with the pregnancy that she would no longer be able to travel. I just thought that the way she was acting was Strange.

"I thought that we could go on and get married and once you leave for Japan, I can stay in Kentucky and have the baby, and then find a job until you get back to the states because I don't want to go overseas," she blurted out. I told her that there was no way that I would miss the birth of my first child, but she continued coming up with excuses, so I simply left her apartment, pissed.

Once I called and gave my mom an update on things, she told me that it sounds obvious that Alyssa was lying about something, and that she believed that either she wasn't pregnant, or she was pregnant by some else. I told my mom that what she had just said sounded ridiculous, but she just went on about how she felt as though this entire thing was going to blow up in my face. She also offered having Alyssa investigated by some folks she knew in Kentucky, but I pleaded with her to leave it alone, so she told me that I was on my own.

I spent a whole week not communicating with Alyssa for I was still pissed off at her for not getting her passport, but I decided to head on to Vegas for a quick "I do" and get on with things. Once we returned, Alyssa immediately wanted to head to Kentucky. I told her that she would have to wait until I was ready to leave. She wanted to hurry up and get home to prove to everyone that she was married. I thought that shit was silly, cause as a newly married woman, why did she need to leave three days after getting hitched? Furthermore, I remembered something MoBo had told me about how all the women were always trying to prove how they could outdo the other just to make the older women, including Alyssa's mom, brag about them. He said that everything they did was like a competition and getting the older ladies' approval was like getting the ultimate prize and trophy. This sounded absurd back when he said it, but for some reason, I started to feel as though this kind of shit was just the beginning of a hole of craziness. I am wondering if I made one of the biggest mistakes of my life.

Chapter Thirteen

Man, once I got to Japan, Alyssa went through more money than I could count; luckily, I had a side job as a bartender at the NCO club. When I requested photos of Alyssa so that I can see how big she was getting, she kept making excuses about how she felt too fat for pictures, so I left it at that. This went on for months, but I let it go, but what concerned me was that she was spending far too much money and not writing or calling as much, and I just decided that the pregnancy was getting to her, until, I received a big envelop from my mom. At first, I thought it was a care package or something because this is what she normally did for me, but, it was a stack of photos, X-rays, and letters.

I was stunned at what I was looking at. Deac and Erb had got with MoBo, and he spilled a whole lot of secrets to them, so they investigated more. Turns out, Alyssa wasn't pregnant when I left the states, and according to the X-rays, she was at least four and a half months pregnant prior to us getting closer, and then, she became pregnant again two months after I had left for Japan. I guess this heifer thought I couldn't do simple math, cause if she got pregnant after I left, how in the hell would she be able to explain it. Not only did she stage this entire event, according to what MoBo stated, this was common practice for all of these ladies, and it was started by their mother's great grandmother and her sisters. The women were known for having what they called, "The Round Table Meetings." During these meetings, all of the women would discuss how they would trap men, especially those in the military, or men that had big money and positions at huge businesses. These women were like vultures, and they all focused more on how they could control their men, paid little to no attention to their children, and always belittled people that they felt were beneath them. Military men were their favorite catch because they felt as though they could control things more because they believed that many of them were vulnerable and easy to control. They also made sure that they had a spare or two, so that they could always have more control and get more money out of them, especially if they could drain their husbands. If by chance any of the men decided to leave the marriage, most of them left with full custody of their children, but the women would still find a way to get money out of the men for as long as they could.

One sister, Bell, married an officer, tried to control him, cheated on him and laughed in his face about everything that she was doing, and ridiculed him in front of people whenever they attended officers' balls, family gatherings, and just about every place they went. She had three sons and two daughters with this guy because not only was he an officer in the military, he also came from a family that had big money and businesses. Bell clung to this man and stripped his pride for at least ten years, and their children attended private schools, and were spoiled rotten, but Bell never showed any motherly behavior towards any of them. But as long as they were excelling in sports, academics, and beauty competitions, she made people think that she was the best mom on earth, but the kids knew better. Bell's husband had a heart attack after he had found some photographs of her and other men having sex, and come to find out, a friend of hers had secretly been taking notes of everything Bell was doing, and had set her up, then she started forwarding photos, letters, and hotel bills to Bell's husband. Bell had befriended Carlotta and thought they she had a true friend that she could meet some of her dates at her house with. But what Bell didn't know is that one of the maids at a hotel was a friend of Carlotta's sister, and she told Carlotta about how her sister's husband had been one of the many regular guys that Bell was seeing there, so she decided to secretly destroy Bell.

Once Bell's husband had confronted her about the contents of the envelop, she laughed in his face and walked out the door and headed to her mom's house to call a special round table meeting. The women agreed that Bell should work this man and bleed him dry until he break and then leave his ass hanging, but keep the kids so that she could continue getting most of his money. At first, Bell was reluctant to keep the kids, but her mom suggested that if she didn't, he could very well change the entire flow of money she would get if the courts had to make a decision, and besides, if she didn't find the envelop and burn it, he would always have something to bring up in court and that could leave her with almost nothing, plus it could be a huge blemish on the reputation of the women in our family. Hedda was the matriarch of the family, which was a position that she did not take lightly, and she ruled with an iron fist, and everybody did anything to satisfy her.

So, after Bell's husband was released from the hospital after being there for a week with no one, not even Bell, coming to visit him, because Bell, didn't say anything to the kids about what had happened to their father, he returned home, and the first thing that Bell said to him was, "Where is that damn envelop?" He looked at her in a shocked manner, and told her that he had no idea. Bell was pissed as hell cause she had torn the house up looking for it, but could night find it anywhere. Instead of her continuing to ask about the envelop, Bell knew at that moment that he had some plans of his own. She was pissed that this weak ass man could try to get smart all of a sudden, but she knew that she had to use Hedda's "Plan B," right away. Bell decided to change and make nice with her husband until Hedda gave the word to try and get rid of him because he had become a serious liability at this point. But, her husband wasn't buying it and he had plans of his own.

One day, Bell arrived home around the time she felt that her husband would be there, but the house was empty. Once she entered their bedroom, she noticed that the closet doors were opened. She immediately viewed the empty closets and went berserk, because she suddenly realized that homeboy was gone. She went to the bedroom safe and found it empty, and to the safe in the dining room, and found it empty. Braxton Forrest had left Bell with nothing, and had finally come to his senses. In the weeks ahead, Bell learned that she had to move from the house, her brand new Mercedes was repossessed, and she could not gain access to their joint checking accounts because Braxton had closed them and had also cut off all of the credit cards. He got his divorce, and the kids decided to remain with their mom, but, the support he sends for them goes through his sister Katie Mae. Bell became delusional, and although she was already diagnosed as being Bi-Polar, now she was a bit out of control to the point where she had to be institutionalized. Bell was allergic to not having money and other stuff that she wanted, and for the last five years, she has been in and out of the nut house.

Bell's downfall didn't have that much of an impact on the round table meetings, in fact, they are as strong as ever. Hedda's round table successor was none other than Alyssa's mom, and she tried to groom her daughters to be powerful, and ruled every inch of their houses and their husbands and future husbands. The round table meetings was filled with women that were self-serving, but what they all failed to understand is that whomever ruled the table, controlled everyone and their mates and their minds, which would obviously be pure ignorance to outsiders, and not even the men and boys of the family could attend these meetings, MoBo and other men found a way to listen in; MoBo discovered the secret meetings by accident, but he never let on that he knew any of the details of its existence to anyone, but other men in the family before him, also found ways to listen in on these meetings. For the most part, a lot of the men stayed away, even though these women were their sisters, cousins, and aunts, they realized that by staying away as much as possible was the best for everyone.

MoBo was more than happy to oblige Deac in his request about the women. According to the report, he wanted to make sure that I understood how serious this issue was and that he really didn't want me to have to continue dealing with so much lies, deceit, and anything bad that could happen, by being with his niece. My mom, Erb, and Deac all suggested that I wait until I finish my tour in Japan, which be six months, because surprising to me, I received a revision of my original orders that changed from three years to eighteen months, and knowing my mom's connections, and Erb and Deac having a lot of pull and friends in high places such as the Masons, and both Erb and Deac had served during the Cuba Missile Crisis, and part of the Vietnam War until 1969. We all agreed that I would return to the states, and act as if I didn't know anything, until I get enough visible evidence to go along with what MoBo gave to them, and especially see who the baby looks like, if there is actually one to be born; I was so puzzled about everything that I couldn't believe that all this shit was happening. Aunt Eunice always told me to keep my ears to the streets, but I folded and let my guard down on this one. She also reminded me that no matter how much we know, how well we keep our noses clean, life will still happen to us because we ain't perfect, and that we have to go through many things throughout our lifetime in order to get through somethings and be able to learn from them and be able to move forward with more motivation to succeed, cause if we don't experience any type of problems in our lives, we either become dumber, weak, or numb to future stuff. I miss those life-learning lessons and great wisdom from Aunt Eunice and even Ms. Duby.

After thinking things through, I cut off all communication with Alyssa and decided that once I return to the states, I would deal with her then. Months passed by, and my mom sent me a picture of what was supposed to be my son, but, even though this was a beautiful gift from above, I could already see none of me in this child. The baby was medium complexion, and had features similar to guy that lived across from Alyssa at her old apartment building. Oh well, the truth will be revealed soon enough.

Chapter Fourteen

When I arrived in Kentucky, I hadn't spoken with Alyssa in almost a year, but I was ready to find out what the hell was going on because this heifer had been getting money from me on a monthly basis, because this was the only money that she was receiving from me until I find out what was really going on. I had changed my accounts prior to leaving the states, to another credit union, so, she didn't have any way of getting to my money. I also learned that MoBo had mentioned that her mom was planning on making Alyssa sue me for money and anything else she could get because she has been taking care of Alyssa and her baby all the while I was in Japan. MoBo also said that her mom knew about everything, but is going to try and play stupid and act like she don't know anything near the truth about what Alyssa did, but that all of them bitches know what's going on.

As soon as Alyssa saw me at the door, she tried to act as if she missed me, and tried to hug me, but I moved away.   Her mom came out of the kitchen looking stupid as ever, with a huge faced smile on her face, and said, "Hey son in-law, we hadn't heard from you in so long that we didn't know if something bad had happened to you." Then she motioned for Alyssa's niece Prudence to go get the baby, and I braced myself for this next part of the act. Meanwhile, Alyssa was still acting like the loving wife and gesturing me to take a seat so that I can meet my son. I looked at everyone in such a cold manner that I couldn't understand why they wanted to continue with this disastrous show.

Prudence brought the baby to me and tried to place him in my arms, and as I looked at the boy, I turned to Alyssa and asked her what the hell did she think would happen once I had seen him. She couldn't say nothing, but her mom had plenty to say. "Well Dee, you know babies tend to look a little funny when they are first born, and in a couple of months, he will be looking just like you," she tried to explain. I stopped all of them in their tracks. I told them bitches that they must really think that I was stupid, because for one thing, that baby was closer to one instead of the amount of months Alyssa had claimed, so she had to have gotten pregnant months after I was in Japan. Furthermore, I told them that the baby looked more like Isaac, Alyssa's old neighbor, and as soon as I said that, Alyssa fell to the floor, balling like a two year-old, and begging me to forgive her. Her mother called her all kinds of ignorant and stupid bitches, and poor Prudence started shaking, almost dropped the baby, then she finally sat down with him. I asked to see the birth certificate, but Alyssa's mom snapped, "Why you concerned about the birth certificate, your name isn't on there and he had my last name." This confirmed all that MoBo had said, but I didn't mention his name at all, in fact, I wanted to find him and meet with him secretly and thank him for all he did.

I told Alyssa, her mom, and anyone else that was listen that I was done, and all I wanted was for her to sign the divorce papers so I can be on my way. Her mom looked at me and was shocked that I mentioned divorce. Alyssa begged me not to leave her, and her mom shouted, "How in the hell you come into my house with some damn divorce papers that Alyssa better not sign or I will break her neck?" I told her that if she didn't sign the papers, right then, and right now, I was going to my lawyer and give him copies of everything from the fake pregnancy test, X-rays, and everything else that I had on her daughter, and the publicity would make her look foolish and I would make sure that everyone of your Big Tea Ladies' members get a copy of all of it. Her mom jerked Alyssa's arm after she had thrown an ink pen at her and shouted, "You dumb ass bitch, sign that damn paper so this fool can get his ass out of my house and out of your life for good!" After I got what I came for and before leaving out of the door, I turned to Alyssa and her mother and told them both that they needed help and I was going to pray for them cause they were going to mess with the wrong person one of these days, but if my family, (Meaning Erb and Deac) had their way, y'all would come up missing, then I left them standing there looking dumbfounded.

Sa looked at me and laughed. "Man, I thought I had dealt with some ignorant and plotting women but this takes the cake," he said. "This shit reminds me of Tadpole and Swamp' little brother Frost." "Frost almost did time for beating the hell out of his wife for cheating on him and video chatting with a dude name Warren Gadson." I told him that I remembered Warren cause he did ten years for popping a cap in Soody and Yank's brother then beating up their mom, after they had ripped him off, and he only got ten years cause he ratted Bone Head, Felon, and Reese out cause you know they had been selling heroin and coke for Tardy Man for the last two years." "Well, anyway, Frost had married Nada Hill after her parents threatened to kill him if he didn't after she got knocked up with their first kid, but this chick was on some serious nympho shit." "Although she was a very attractive woman, in her mind, she thought that all she needed was her looks to get what she wanted from men, but, these guys didn't realize the health issues they would face later." "Frost said all she did was sit around the house on the phone telling all her business to her so-called friends, and the kids would be hungry and smelling like piss until he came home, and he had to cook, cause you know he was a cook in the Army for fifteen years. "She would leave the house right after the kids were fed and cleaned by Frost, and would be gone for hours, one day, he got a babysitter and called Sully to come go with him so he could follow her in his car so she wouldn't recognize it. Man, this woman was messing around with Warren, who didn't have a job, was staying with his sister Melinda, and was obviously getting money from Nada, and a few other women he was playing." Wow, that's some deep shit, so what happened after that.

"Man, after he found out about Warren, he went home and Sully helped him hack into her computer and found out that she had been emailing and chatting with not only Warren, but other men and doing sex acts for them in many of the videos." "So, he got Sully's girlfriend Twyla to get more friendly with Nada and find out where else she was getting the money, and man, Twyla said that Nada had been hooking on the side for Warren and hanging around his other five women, and also going into Frost's secret bank account and bought Warren the latest Buick he has been driving lately." Frost was so pissed, that he waited for her to come home one night, and soon as she came in, he started beating on that ass, and it just so happened that after he had broken her nose and jaw, Craig Stevens had stopped by to pay Frost some money that he owed him, and Craig was the one that saved Nada's life that night, cause he pried Frost off of her and made him leave with him. Nada never reported Frost, but she did have to go to the hospital, and she told the police that somebody had attacked her when she was coming home, and they obviously believed her cause they never asked any more questions. Frost, however, left that bitch and took his kids to live with his aunt, and Nada ended up being found at Warren's house after she suspiciously overdosed on heroin laced with rat poison, but the real story is that Warren found out that he had a serious disease, and the rumor was that it was AIDS, so he and his other girls offed Nada."

That was some wild shit man, I told Sa. These women out here on a serious hustle to get what they want, but many of them fail to play by anybody's rules and they come up short in the end. But I finally found a woman that I thought I would marry, but she ended up being too damn fake as well as needy, and she wanted to cling to me too much. Her name was Jazmyn Dixon and she was from Nebraska. I had never met a woman from Nebraska that I wanted to date, but this girl was totally packing. But, after about four months in, I decided to turn her loose cause this woman acted like she was my mother, my boss, and she was so stuck on herself that I let her go. She didn't take it very well, and she kept calling and stopping by, but eventually, she finally got the message. Then I hooked up with this girl name Moneta, and she ended up lying to me about being pregnant because I had no intentions of marrying her cause she really wasn't the type of woman that acted like she wanted to be married and have kids. We got along really good in the beginning, but after almost a year, she started pushing me towards making up my mind to marry her, and it was a real turn off for me, especially since my first marriage turned out to be hell. So, she gave me an ultimatum and I told her that although I cared a lot about her, I didn't want to get married again, so she bounced. She didn't even contact after learning that she had orders for Korea, so, I let it go, and focused on my job. But, after she returned from Korea, she got in touch with me through Sergeant King's wife, and I met up with her at a restaurant downtown. She came clean and told me that she had to leave Korea early cause she was pregnant with my child and that she wasn't planning on telling me about him, but her mom told her that I needed to know. I looked at her with a blank face as I thought about how my ex-wife had tricked me about having my baby. I asked where the baby was, and she motioned for this teen-aged girl to come to our table who had been holding a baby, and when I looked at him, I saw me all over him. I looked at her and she told me that she wanted me to raise him because she couldn't have any more kids and that she didn't really want to be a mother. I told her to meet me at the clinic on Tuesday and once I got the results of the blood test, it proofed that I was the father, so, I had his last name changed to mine because she had already named him after me, and I took him to see my mom, and she helped me out by taking him and keeping him until I was settled and ready to take over, and he has been with me ever since. Moneta sends birthday cards, money, and cloths to my mom's house for him, but frankly, I don't want her to do anything for him because he needs her love and presence, not money and resents, but, he's doing fine, and I don't say negative things to him about her around him, so he's good. I do ask if he wants to see her, and he told me that if she wanted to be in his life and act like a real mother, then he might want to see her from time to time, but since she doesn't make any effort to, then he's good because the ball was in her court, but for now, he has me and my mom.

"Man, you good, but I would not let her send nothing or talk to him at all, in fact, she would be dead to me," Sa said. Well, Sa, she is and will always be his mom cause we can't choose the parents that we get, but we can try and not make the same mistakes that they do. "You right Dee, but that is so cruel to do something like that to a child, especially as their mom., Sa said."

Chapter Fifteen

Finally, I was retired from the Army, had my lil man with me, and life was good, at least for now. I sit back, often looking back at the past, and wonder if things could have turned out any different for me, especially had my dad lived. Never getting the chance to be around your dad growing leaves such a heavy void in your life, no matter how others who are close to you try to fill that gap; that is a space that can't ever be filled, by any man.

One day, as I met my mom in Ohio at the house that Aunt Eunice had lived in, she told me that she had some interesting things to show me. I wondered what all of this was about, but I prepared myself for the worse, hoping that it turned out not so bad.

She showed me the first diary that I remember seeing her with after Aunt Eunice gave it to her long before she had passed away. This diary had names in it that I had never heard of, and it also contained newspaper clippings, dates written in red, and I had no idea what it all meant. My mom started decoding everything for me by opening up another diary that had more names and marriage, birth, and death certificates in it. Then there was a huge box of old pictures and magazines.

In order to understand Aunt Eunice's book, we had to match up dates with another book I immediately wanted to know who the other book belonged to and why did Aunt Eunice have it. We stumbled across an old photograph of a beautiful woman, sitting on a porch and another one of the same woman with a man and woman in it. Suddenly, my mom looked at me as if she had solved a mystery puzzle. She told me that if I stared hard enough, I could see who these women are. I didn't see nothing that gave me a glue. She shook her head, and said, "This is Ms. Duby, and the other photo is Ms. Duby and Aunt Eunice, but I don't know who this man is." Looking at the photos again, it suddenly looked like Ms. Duby and Aunt Eunice, but all I could do is ask why are they in these photos together, and why hadn't we ever seen these. I had more questions faster than I could get an answer. Just then, we heard Erb come. He looked at us in a strange and weird way as if he thought that we had learned a big secret or something. "Hey babies, what going on," he said. My mom didn't say nothing, she just looked at him, and he gave her this strange back as if he had got caught with his hand in the cookie jar. "Hey Dee, how ya doing man?" he asked. I returned the greeting, as he came closer to see what we were doing.

"So, you finally opened up all that stuff that Eunice had, huh? He asked. "Well, I knew this day would eventually come, and yes, I am your father," he said. My mom stood straight up and shouted, "What!" "I thought you had gone through everything and learned the truth about all of us," he said with a puzzled look on his face. I sat there, frozen with disbelieve, shock, and confusion.

"Eunice's real name was Betty Andrews," he explained as he picked up the newspaper clipping where it showed her behind bars for murdering a White man and his wife when she was around twenty-three, and even though it was self-defense, back in those days, Blacks was still in the wrong. His wife had been sleeping with Betty's husband, and one day she came home and caught both of them in bed, her bed, and she beat the woman so bad, that by the time she ran home and told her old man that Betty just jumped on her because she asked her if she could make her a sweet potato pie, which was a damn lie, old man Withers decided to catch Betty in her back yard while she was hanging cloths out to dry, and when he grabbed her, she broke free and picked up a rake and beat his ass to a pulp; Betty was a brutal fighting woman, but only if she was threatened, cause she was one of the nicest people you could ever meet. So his son Roy Boy and his wife came after Betty, and Winston Jones punched him in the face while Betty kicked Mrs. Withers in the stomach so hard, that she fell on a rusty nail that was sticking up from the ground and it went deep into her neck. By this time, there were so many folks watching the whole thing, and Jeb Branch ran out and saw what had happened and he told the sheriff that Betty had killed them dead. She only spent about two years in jail, cause Mr. Withers' son Bronson talked the sheriff into letting her go cause he had no real proof that she did anything cause he was only going by the White's word and didn't listen to nothing the colored folks had to say. Bronson remembered how Betty saved him from Clint Edwards boys years ago, and Bronson wasn't his father's favorite son and had been treated like a retarded person all of his life, so he helped Betty, and after they released her, he warned her to leave and go to another state and don't return 'cause a lot of the White folks' would try to get her. So, once she had made it to Ohio, she started hooking at a brothel that was owned by My dad's sister in-law Katie Mae, who also just turned out to be Betty's sister that she thought she would never see again. And Ms. Duby was one of the cooks at the brothel that got pregnant by this big time hustler named Race Andrews, and they got married to keep him from going to jail, but by the time your mom, was born, he was killed by an e partner of him called Slick Will cause he made far more money and had more smarts than Slick did. I took over the business, then I married your mom when she turned fifteen and was pregnant with you.

Your mother was one of the most beautiful women I had ever laid my eyes on, but being raised up in the type of environment we did, hustling of all kinds had its price and many folks came up missing if they run into folks that wasn't trustworthy. Every man wanted her, and she wanted all the money and things they had to offer. She never had to work as a prostitute or nothing, but the men would swarm around her everywhere she went. We didn't stay together that long after we were married, no more than two years, cause once she saw that she could get whatever she wanted, from whomever, she claimed that hustle. She had so many women that envied her, and one day, this whore name Hattie got with her girl Judy, and they trapped her inside a bathroom at Rooster's Place and had Norton Sayers to bash her head in and it killed her. Once Ms. Duby and Betty got the word, they found all three, hiding out at Paul Tate's house and beat the hell out of Judy and Hattie, but since Norton had fallen asleep, it was easy for them to beat him to a pulp with a cast iron skillet, but before they left, me and Deac made them leave, and after that night, nobody ever heard from nether one of them to this day, and trust e, they never will.

Now, when he explained how Ms. Duby fit in, he told us that Ms. Duby's real name was Eunice and she allowed Betty to use her name because by the time things got hot with everybody who was in the hustling game or close to anyone in the game, shit got hot and we had to go underground for a long time and change our names. But when we came back on the scene, we were ready for anything. "I may not be too proud of a whole lot of stuff that y'all will never know about, trust and believe me when I tell you that, we protect our own, no matter who or what," Erb stated. He also stated that Deac was my mother's brother, and the old man that I used to run into by the bridge, Old Man Carson was my uncle on Erb dad's side of the tree, and he wasn't homeless either. Turns out, this dude had a mini mansion down on Blythe Rd, but he pretends to be homeless in order to reach a lot of the young folk and try to instill some knowledge in them. Man, I thought to myself, lies and deceit has been an ongoing practice in this family. But, now that Erb, or should I say Granddad, spent half the night clearing everything up and revealing all these secrets to us, I believe that my mom understood like I did, why they covered up so much, because like he said, they had to do what had to be done to protect all of us, and they are still doing that job today. The next morning, my mom and I went to see Ms. Duby She met us at the door and told us to

126

come in. She had us believe that this was her house, but, turns out, she owned everything that Eunice had left, but, legally, everything was still in my mom's name. She finished bringing us up to speed about the past and also told us that she has been living in the big house in the back portion, ever since it was built, but since we never really went back there, we had no idea that she was living back there. She walked across the way with us and we entered through the side door and as we entered the back part of the humongous house, all I saw was every picture of me, my mom, Erb, and a few other folks on the mantle.

Well, this trip home wasn't that bad, and I learned a whole lot more than I could ever have imagined. But, just when I thought that all was well, Erb comes and tell us that Rocky Henderson's body shot up in the park down on Weston, and that word on the streets is that this prostitute that just arrived on the scene from California, called Candy K did it because he was trying to force her inside Midget Green's car. He had been order by Midget to clean up Banks and Weston Streets before the next morning, which meant that he needed to scoop up all the independent whores on the streets so that he could add them to his stable, but home girl wasn't having it. So, Deac found her hiding in the alley behind the laundry mat on Kale Court, so, he called Erb, and Erb got her out of there and she's caught a flight back to California about before noon today. The only way that Erb and Deac would go out of their way for unknown people is when they know that their rival hustlers are looking for them, so if they can find them first, they get them out and to a safe place. Boy, the game of hustling gets crazier and crazier at times, but I see why people with good sense stay close to their own homes.

Lies come in all shades of the color rainbow, but, no matter what the color of lies are, whether blue, black, white, green, whatever, if the hustle of whatever game you laying in lack substance and can cause harm to you or those close to you, then you playing in the wrong corners of the game. Everyone has a hustle, but not everyone will come out on top or nor even close to the middle. When your hustle consists of activity the can eliminate others through self-serving results, bad deeds, revenge and envy, sooner or later you can be swallowed up and sink fast and hard, or slow and painful no matter who you are. In today's society, I look out and see many of the young folks burning fast and don't even realize it. Back when I was growing up, respect for others, especially older people, got you much farther and allowed the most unusual people to come to your rescue whenever you were caught up in some real shit. The society before me was even better from what I'm told by my elders, cause everybody knew who their people were, and they took care of one another at the drop of a dime. But now, I have witnessed so many senseless crimes, murders, assaults, and other crazy events occur that has become expected, but still amaze me and has started to occur more often than necessary. What used to be known as hick towns that had none to very low crime rates, has turned into places where you have to locked your doors, keep your weapons on the ready, and be cautious of people who turns out to be the children and grandchildren of people you grew up around.

Now, high crime is occurring in any type of city and state in the nation, and just like bullets when they are fired, crime doesn't have any name or place on it, for everyone are moving targets no matter who we are, because the hustle of the game in this reality, is so clouded with madness that at any given moment, someone, somewhere, will be snapping on somebody for any given reason.

The flow of hustle is full of lies in the actions of many folk, and that includes many hustlers in the church, in the prison, out in the streets, in the schools, in the world of business, and your home, and just about everything you do. But whatever your hustle is, make it more profitable for the benefit of not only you, but for those who you are responsible for, and for those coming up after you have gone on and retired. Hustling itself isn't always bad, for if you are on a hustle to do good and help others, whether you help the needy through nonprofit organizations, help train others so that they can help themselves, or simply get your hustle on through working towards a degree so that you can get a better job, make it without the help of lies that can resurface and blemish the entire work that could possibly turn out to be something phenomenal.

A Few Words from The Author

No matter who we are, what we do or don't do, life can be filled with loads of crazy moments. We live in a society that consist of many complexed situations that finds us at our lowest to highest points, but we have to continue to make adequate changes to our hustle. The game of any hustle has many rules, and as humans, we must keep our eyes, ears, and minds wide open and our mouth closed more often than we do so that we don't get eaten alive by our own ignorance of greed, limited knowledge, and lack of motivation to make changes to what we do. *D. L. Reynolds*

BLUE LIES

(Reality Changes the Hustle of the Game)

By
D. L. Reynolds